Acknowled

CW01502109

Thank you to everyone who helped me with information and hints on sources; you made the doodlebug summer and after come alive for me. So many hints and tips, including Karen A'Court's message: "Did you know my mother-in-law grew up in Antwerp during the war?" and Carole Tucker's remark about how small children could often hear approaching doodlebugs ahead of the adults (as she could). People were so generous in offering help and information; Joy Hilder gave me her copy of her vivid account of the Otford V1. Mark and Diana Miller gave me more material about the V1 that landed at the end of my road, and neighbours added to this at one of the street parties.

The Home Front History group on Facebook provided some particularly interesting insights. John Bull, former colleague and now friend, has sent links to a treasure trove of material, with regular messages and tips. His mother Doreen volunteered to tell me all about wartime Christmas meals, rationing and the reality of what was available; it was invaluable to have a first-hand account. Jenny A'Court did a wonderful job with her description of everyday life in Antwerp, very evocative and quite terrifying once you read between the lines (those luggage labels for the children!). Jeffrey Hobbs generously shared his late mother's first-hand account of the Oldham bombing with me.

I would like to thank Pieter Serrien for his painstaking research where he listed those who died in the Rex Cinema, Antwerp:

A special thank you to Marc Canillas for all his help. It has been a real pleasure to be able to share the same interests and debate obscure research points; we have looked at WW2, especially the doodlebug campaign, together. I am particularly grateful for his help in resolving the puzzle of the Aldwych casualty figures!

I should also like to thank my friends, especially Julia Wright, Clare Gibson (and Katie), Ann Brueckner White, Roz Cooke, Michelle Bailey and Pat Perry for their help and support and their willingness to discuss the book. My cousins Gilly Sanders and Hilary Mawson have always been supportive and have provided practical help and encouragement on many occasions. Thanks also to Marcia Hughes and friends at the Landmark and to my neighbour Hazel Harrison, who provided invaluable technical support on several occasions, including lending me her spare mouse at a time of crisis.

My special thanks to my son, Alan, for all his help, including his thoughtful critique of my section on how a V1 works. His "peregrine falcon, should you have one to hand" analogy was particularly appreciated. His sense of humour, technical and historical insights and excellent IT skills have been invaluable and contributed a great deal to the overall work. This book is dedicated to him.

Every effort has been made to trace copyright holders and I should like to thank all those who have kindly granted permission to use quoted material. Any errors or omissions that persist are my responsibility alone.

THE V1
FLYING BOMB
CAMPAIGN
— 1944-1945 —

THE DOODLEBUG
SUMMER *and* AFTER

JAN GORE

Pen & Sword
MILITARY

AN IMPRINT OF PEN & SWORD BOOKS LTD.
YORKSHIRE - PHILADELPHIA

First published in Great Britain in 2024 by
PEN AND SWORD MILITARY
An imprint of
Pen & Sword Books Limited
Yorkshire – Philadelphia

ISBN 978 1 39906 581 8

Typeset in Times New Roman 12/16 by
SJmagic DESIGN SERVICES, India.
Printed and bound in the UK by CPI Group (UK) Ltd.

Pen & Sword Books Limited incorporates the imprints of Atlas, Archaeology,
Aviation, Discovery, Family History, Fiction, History, Maritime, Military,
Military Classics, Politics, Select, Transport, True Crime, Air World,
Frontline Publishing, Leo Cooper, Remember When, Seaforth Publishing,
The Praetorian Press, Wharncliffe Local History, Wharncliffe Transport,
Wharncliffe True Crime and White Owl.

For a complete list of Pen & Sword titles please contact
PEN & SWORD BOOKS LIMITED
George House, Units 12 & 13, Beevor Street, Off Pontefract Road,
Barnsley, South Yorkshire, S71 1HN, England
E-mail: enquiries@pen-and-sword.co.uk
Website: www.pen-and-sword.co.uk

or

PEN AND SWORD BOOKS
1950 Lawrence Rd, Havertown, PA 19083, USA
E-mail: uspen-and-sword@casematepublishers.com
Website: www.penandswordbooks.com

MIX
Paper | Supporting
responsible forestry
FSC® C013604

Contents

Introduction

Ever since my mother had mentioned that some of her friends went to the Guards' Chapel "and never came back", I had been intrigued and increasingly fascinated by the stories of the V1s. I researched the incident, helped with the 70th anniversary commemoration at the Chapel in 2014, and later wrote a book about what happened that day on 18 June 1944. But the stories haunted me and during lockdown I began to look at information relating to the wartime events in my area of Southwest London. I realised that the ten-week "doodlebug summer" was far from the whole story and the V1 incidents were a thread that ran though suburban life, just as much as they did in daily life in central London. The air launches proved a significant part of the V1 campaign; they meant that doodlebugs could continue to appear apparently randomly, most notably on Christmas Eve in the Manchester area.

I also looked at the use of V1s in Antwerp and elsewhere – a terrible campaign that deserves to be better known.

This book tells the story of the V1 campaign, its development and what happened in June 1944 and after. I have tried to tell the stories of those who lived through these times, in London and elsewhere; it is clear from their testimony that the doodlebugs were a terrifying element of everyday life and one that deserves to be remembered.

Chapter 1

The Very Start of the Doodlebug Campaign

As the German invasion of Poland began on 1 September 1939, Britain waited tensely to see what would happen about the British ultimatum to Germany. Children were starting to be evacuated that weekend; trains from major cities were taking them away from areas of danger, school by school. (My fifteen-year-old father left London with his school for Godalming and would not return to live with his parents for the rest of the war. Just one schoolchild among many, but his account helped me to realise some of the disruption involved, even for those too young to fight.) Nine major roads out of London were made one-way for several days so that there was no hindrance to evacuation and other traffic leaving London.

On Sunday 3 September 1939 the ultimatum expired, and Neville Chamberlain spoke to the nation to announce that Britain was at war. That same month, on 19 September, Hitler talked in Danzig about "a weapon that cannot be used against us". R.V. Jones, who had recently joined the Directorate of Scientific Research and was attached to Air Intelligence, started trying to establish what this could be. Was it a veiled threat? He asked Frederick "Bimbo" Norman, a professor of German from King's College London and now a colleague, to look at the translation. Was it a mystery weapon? The Foreign Office translators had implied that it was a specific weapon ("Waffe") against which no defence could avail. However, the word could also be translated as "force" as in a whole armed service, for example the Luftwaffe, Hitler's air force. Dr Jones thought it most likely that Hitler was referring to his own air force at that point.

He was asked to search the files of the Secret Intelligence Service to see whether he could establish what the mystery weapon could be. He compiled a list of possible weapons, which was completed on 11 November 1939. These included:

1) Bacterial warfare
2) New gases
3) Flame weapons
4) Gliding bombs, aerial torpedoes and pilotless aircraft
5) Long range guns and rockets
6) New torpedoes, mines and submarines
7) Death rays, engine-stopping rays and magnetic guns

Perhaps fortunately, during this latest war bacterial warfare and gases were not involved, nor was option 7, although people were issued with gas masks that they had to carry with them, and the tops of pillar boxes were painted with special gas-detecting paint in a yellowish green. If poison gas was present in the air the square of paint changed colour, to alert the public to a gas attack. The type of gas expected was mustard gas, one of a range of gases used in trench warfare in World War One. The mere possibility of gas attacks in WW2 was quite a powerful psychological weapon, especially for those who remembered accounts of its effects in the previous war. (Allegedly 10 million gas masks were ordered by Neville Chamberlain as early as 1937.)

The "Oslo Report" was a three-inch thick parcel left by a "well-wishing German scientist" at the British Legation in Norway in November 1939. It did not mention pilotless aircraft specifically but said that the Germans had begun a major programme of long-range rocket development; they were carrying out research at a place called Peenemünde on the island of Usedom in the Baltic. This name would appear again later in the war and prove to be significant.

In March 1942 the Argus company contacted the Air Ministry in Berlin to see if they were still interested in pilotless planes; this concept had been considered in the past. Field-Marshal Erhard Milch, who was in charge of all Luftwaffe aircraft production, was very interested and he took the decision to go ahead. He met Robert Lusser, a talented aircraft designer, on 28 May 1942. Milch became aware of the idea's potential and made the work high priority.

Robert Lusser (1899-1969) was born in Ulm. He trained as an aeronautical engineer and took his degree in 1928; he was also an aviator. He worked for Heinkel and then moved to Messerschmidt in Augsburg, where he became chief of design and designed the Me 109, among others. He returned to Heinkel and designed the first jet engine to fly. After that he went to Fieseler, where he became involved with the company's attempts to produce a pilotless aircraft, initially named the Fi-103 (also the FZG-76). This was a collaborative effort between Fieseler and the engine manufacturer Argus, who were developing a pulsejet engine. Lusser joined forces with Fritz Gosslau from the Argus engine works to work on the design.

(A little background history: the Lusser family lived in Kassel 1941-1944, but there were constant air raids. Eventually the area was fire-bombed, and they had to leave the city. They escaped to Bavaria where Hildegard Lusser and all five children lived in one room in a farmhouse. On 13 March 1945, US bombers came over the Alps and dropped a bomb. It was a direct hit and Hildegard was killed. Robert Lusser, who had been working in Berlin, left to care for his children in Bavaria. This meant that he was in the US zone at the end of the war. The Americans asked him to join them, and in 1948 the family moved to the US where he worked as an inventor and taught in an engineering school; he was always designing. Later he worked for and eventually led Messerschmidt. He remarried and had four more children.)

It was Robert Lusser and Fritz Gosslau who developed the V1 flying bomb. The name came from *Vergeltungswaffe* - "revenge weapon". The design was originally in competition with Wernher von Braun's V2 vertical take-off rocket, but it was decided both designs should be developed. Lusser and von Braun were rivals, and even later their relationship was never frictionless.

On 27 February 1942, Lusser and Gosslau sketched out the design of an aircraft with the pulsejet above the tail, the basis for the future V1. The preliminary design was complete by early April 1942 and was submitted to the Luftwaffe on 5 June 1942, where it became a firm project. The specifications included a range of 299 km (186 miles), a speed of 700 km/h (435 mph), and it was capable of delivering a 500-kilogram (½-long-ton) warhead. Project Fieseler Fi 103 was approved on 19 June and assigned the code name *Kirschkern* (cherry stone) and the cover name *Flakzielgerat* 76 (FZG-76) (FZG=anti-aircraft apparatus). Flight tests then began at the Luftwaffe's coastal test centre at Peenemünde West on the Baltic coast.

Meanwhile, the Allied raids on Lübeck and Rostock in March and April 1942 had a further effect; they persuaded Hitler to decide on a policy of retaliation, starting with the Baedeker raids of April-June 1942. Ultimately it would lead to the use of the V weapons.

The V1's maiden flight took place on 23 December 1942 from Peenemünde. By then it had an 1830lb warhead and a 182-gallon fuel tank which meant it could last about 30 minutes: plenty of time to reach London from the Pas de Calais. It was 26 feet long, with a wingspan of up to 18 feet, a range of 150 miles and a maximum speed of 410 mph. The guidance system was crude; it was launched from a "ski site" catapult ramp, and powered by an Argus duct as the propulsion unit did not give sufficient thrust until the bomb reached flying speed. Otherwise, the short wings (needed for ease of handling) would mean a high stalling speed. Once it was airborne, the autopilot then engaged and this regulated both height and speed. (About 20% of all launchings proved defective.) The work on the design continued throughout 1942; it was originally hoped that it would be ready by the end of 1943.

Meanwhile the first prototype V2 rockets were fired on 3 October 1942. Over the next months there were a few more intelligence reports about them which continued into spring 1943. On 19 April 1943 the Central Interpretation Unit at RAF Medmenham was asked to look out for signs of a long-range rocket gun, a remotely-controlled rocket aircraft and "some sort of tube out of which a rocket could be squirted". Meanwhile Duncan Sandys, Churchill's son-in-law and Parliamentary Secretary to the Ministry of Supply, was asked to undertake a special investigation, codenamed "Bodyline".

On 24 April there was a meeting at Medmenham; as a result, Duncan Sandys was convinced the threat was a real one. He immediately ordered further surveys of Peenemünde from the reconnaissance squadron at RAF Benson. On 17 May he gave an interim report to the War Cabinet, in which he suggested that a long-range rocket was probably being developed along with some other type of airborne rocket and he strongly recommended that intelligence sources intensify their search for evidence of a secret weapon.

On 26 May 1943 at Peenemünde, Germany, an A-4 rocket and a flying bomb were tested in front of Hermann Göring, Erhard Milch, and other top German leaders. The A-4 rocket flew perfectly, while the flying bomb crashed after only a mile or two of flight. Nevertheless, it was recommended that both weapons should be developed further.

In June 1943, a couple of agents' reports were received from foreign construction workers at Peenemünde. Specifically, on 22 June there was talk of "winged" rockets, remote-controlled and launched by catapults. The RAF made several reconnaissance sorties on 12 and 23 June to take photographs of the area. One of Constance Babington Smith's fellow interpreters, André Kenny, made the first identification of two V2 long-range rockets lying on road vehicles at Peenemünde. At the same time, Constance Babington Smith was briefed to look out for "anything queer". When she looked at the photographs from 23 June, she remembered the name of Peenemünde from the previous year, although she would require more information before she could provide a positive identification of a V1. By the end of June V2 long-range rockets had been identified for the first time from photographs of the area.

Sandys sent his report to the Cabinet Defence Committee (Operations). They agreed to check Northern France for evidence of any suspicious works and to attack Peenemünde. At this stage, they acknowledged that there might be not one but two secret weapons being developed: a rocket projectile known as A.4 (the V2) and a pilotless aircraft known as Phi.7 (the V1).

In the moonlit early morning of 18 August 1943, Bomber Command carried out a massive attack on Peenemünde. This was called "Operation Hydra" and marked the start of the strategic bombing campaign against the V-weapon programme. The raid hit the housing estate near the test site, including the camp that housed foreign labourers; tragically, the deaths included some of the people who had tried to get information to the British at great risk to themselves. 600 foreign workers were killed, compared with only 130 German scientists and engineers. The raid probably delayed the rocket programme by between four weeks and six months, but the flying bomb work was hardly affected. However, the delays meant that the rocket could not be used simultaneously with the flying bomb in 1944, at least for the first months of the V1 campaign. Instead, the V1 had to be used first.

Between 22 and 28 August 1943 the Germans were carrying out tests, using air launches to drop fuelled missiles. On the first day of testing, a former Danish naval officer spotted an object in a field on Bornholm; this turned out to be a small pilotless aircraft, a research model V1, which had been air-launched from a Heinkel 111. (This is one of the first references to air-launched flying bombs.) It was being tested over the Baltic Sea when it crashed. The officer photographed it and made drawings and descriptions. These were passed to London for further analysis.

From August 1943, the German military were working on three different aspects of the V1 scheme: producing the missiles, training the crews to fire them and building the launch sites. Some changes in design were involved and a higher specification was decided upon; these could not be made ready until February of the following year. It was hard to produce the control gear and diving mechanism because of Allied air attacks at the Fieseler Werke at Kassel, where these were being made. Training the crews was easier than producing the missiles; the troops became Flak Regiment 155(W) and Max Wachtel was their commanding officer. This became part of Army Corps LXV from 15 December 1943. They were based at St Germain, near Paris, which was then a safe distance from the Channel coast and any Allied attacks. By 23 September 1943 40,000 "foreign construction workers" (also more realistically known as "slave labourers") were assigned to build the launch sites; 96 of these sites were planned along the 140 miles of the French coastline, between Calais and the Seine, with two storage bunkers. Fifty-eight of the first 64 were planned to be ready by the end of November 1943.

Tens of thousands of civilians from occupied Europe were forced to make the V-weapons, both V1 and V2, from autumn 1943 onwards. They included a range of nationalities: Russians, Poles, French, Germans, Czechs, Hungarian Jews, Gypsies, Italians, Belgians, Yugoslavs, Dutch and others. Much of this work was done in a huge underground complex known as the *Mittelwerk*, which the Nazis set up after Allied bombing disrupted V2 operations at Peenemünde. The *Mittelwerk* occupied large tunnels underneath a mountain near Nordhausen in the Harz Mountains in central Germany. When the Allies destroyed V1 factories in bombing raids, flying bomb production also moved to the *Mittelwerk*. The prisoners were subjected to a brutal regime, which included starvation, torture and frequent executions while working for the Nazis. As many as 20,000 labourers died as a result. Those working at the V1 sites along the French coast tended to be French, Belgian or Dutch. (More slave labourers died making the V-weapons than the Allied civilians later killed by the doodlebugs during the V1 campaign.)

On 10 September the chiefs of staff agreed that Duncan Sandys should focus on looking at evidence relating to the rocket, while the Air Ministry should collect information about the flying bomb. Four days later, Dr R.V. Jones from the Air Intelligence Branch issued a special note which suggested there were indications that the use of pilotless aircraft could be fairly imminent; the long-range rocket was also being developed.

On 21 September 1943, Churchill made his first guarded reference to the threat. Speaking in the House of Commons he talked about the German leaders' "mysterious allusions to new methods and new weapons which will presently be tried against us". While he admitted it could be rumour-mongering "there is probably more in it than that". A few days later, on 25 September, Dr R V Jones wrote to chiefs of staff: "It is probable that the German Air Force has been developing a pilotless aircraft for long-range bombardment in competition with the rocket and it is very possible that the aircraft will arrive first."

Using signals intercept, British intelligence was able to decipher the results of all the test runs of the flying bombs, as these were sent by an easily broken code. The British could tell that the speed was about 400 mph, while the height ranged between 1,000 and 6,000 feet. More worryingly the test flights showed their accuracy was increasing; it was becoming essential that the launch sites should be located and (ideally) destroyed.

On 23 October the RAF launched an attack on Kassel, where the pilot series of flying bombs was being manufactured at the Fieseler Works. This forced the evacuation of the site and the supply of flying bombs to the test site at Peenemünde was halted between October 1943 and February 1944. In November it was felt by the Germans that another 150 bombs would have to be tested before the trial results would be satisfactory. The start of the campaign against London had to be delayed yet again. The V1 flying bomb was still not ready for operational use, but its accuracy and reliability were continuing to improve.

On 28 October 1943 Duncan Sandys ordered the whole area of north-west France within a 150-mile radius of London to be re-photographed. This involved a hundred separate sorties, but swiftly brought results.

Soon afterwards, in early November, the first "ski site" was spotted, so named because the layout of the storage chamber buildings looked rather like a ski on its side, long and narrow but curved gently at one end. All the ski sites had "a long platform pointing towards London". By 8 November, the team at RAF Medmenham had discovered nineteen sites under construction; two days later they had found twenty-six. On 13 November, for the first time, Section Officer Constance Babington Smith was asked by Wing Commander Kendall to look for something specific: a very small aircraft. She retrieved and checked the photographs she had seen in June; sure enough, they included a midget aircraft. She began to check for more. By 22 November the total of sites had risen to ninety-five. "The most imminent cross-Channel threat... was going to be a flying bomb".

Another set of photos revealed a sort of ramp, holding a tiny cruciform shape on rails: a flying bomb being prepared for launch. On 1 December Constance Babington Smith looked at the "strange structures", previously tentatively identified as "dredging equipment"; she realised that this could be "a catapult for pilotless aircraft".

Destroying the launch sites became a priority before the flying bombs were launched in earnest. This was given the codename Operation Crossbow. The first attack was on 16 December, near Abbeville; it was not accurate enough to destroy the site, however. Meanwhile the construction of ski sites continued; the launch points were on the Pas de Calais and the Somme/Seine areas, and every single "ski ramp" pointed towards London. There could be little mistake as to the intended target. Intelligence reports suggested that flying bombs were already arriving on site to be assembled; agents' reports suggested that each site had a square building that contained no metal. The experts concluded that this meant that whatever was in the square building needed to be free from magnetism, suggesting that the bomb had some form of sensitive compass steering. The assembly routine appeared to involve having the rocket tube already assembled, adding the wings in a small building near the ski site and then launching the rocket via the ramp.

Lord Cherwell wrote to the Prime Minister warning that the first missiles they had located in France might be launched in the next one to three months, if the rate of construction continued. On 14 December, the Deputy Chief of the Air Staff sent out an even more alarming report, warning the Prime Minister that work on the first twenty sites could be completed by early January 1944, and the remainder by February. Most of the launch points were oriented on London but some of the sites in the Cherbourg area were now oriented on Bristol. Dr Jones wrote a report just before Christmas 1943 in which he reported that the flying bombs were not yet ready as technical problems were holding them up. Nevertheless, by then he was able to give the approximate dimensions and range, and to state that the bombs were driven by Argus tube propulsion and came to the ski sites already fuelled from the base depots.

An agent in France was told about a goods wagon containing some unusually shaped crates that had been passing through Rouen. He was able to gain access and measure up the mystery objects; meanwhile other agents were reporting the arrival of yet more of these objects. Some were already being assembled.

The code name changed to "Crossbow" on 27 November and the Air Force gave their new targets the name "No Ball" sites, amid some ribaldry from the airmen. The Allied Expeditionary Air Force had recently been set up under Air Chief Marshal Sir Trafford Leigh-Mallory; it absorbed part of Fighter Command and the rest was renamed Air Defence of Great Britain. Air Marshal Roderic Hill was now in command of this. (He was renowned for visiting various airfields in his own personal Tempest V and carried out 62 anti-V1 patrols himself.)

Leigh-Mallory was ordered to attack the "no ball" sites with bombers of the Allied Expeditionary Air Force, reinforced by heavy bombers of the US Eighth Air Force, whenever the weather precluded attacks on Germany. The American government reacted swiftly to offer support and gave top priority to establishing ways of demolishing the ski sites. On 12 January 1944 General Marshall ordered the Army Air Forces to give top priority to attacking the launch sites and to establish the best methods of doing so. Two weeks later General "Hap" Arnold ordered Brigadier General Grandison Gardner to get "the job done in days not weeks". Once they had devised a strategy, General Gardner and his team flew to England to demonstrate the new method of destroying ski sites.

Attacks on the sites had begun on 5 December, but it soon became apparent that this would not be an easy mission. The bombs they were carrying made the Typhoons and Hurricanes slow to manoeuvre and vulnerable to attack from the ground, while the concrete launching ramps and storage buildings provided very small targets that required a direct hit to destroy. The sites were also heavily defended. The Germans chose areas that had perfect cover, ideally in a small wood near a hard road. They also picked more domestic sites, such as apple and pear orchards, or even village back gardens. It was extremely hard to attack these sites without significant collateral damage to the village's inhabitants.

Bombing at night was less dangerous, at least in theory, but also less accurate – and accuracy was key to the mission's success. On 16 December, near Abbeville, nine Lancasters, led by Wing Commander Leonard Cheshire, delivered all their bombs within 150 yards of the target, but this was still not close enough to do serious damage. On 21 December the American daylight squadrons began to attack, with the bombing reaching a crescendo on Christmas Eve. By then they were using as many as 1,300 aircraft and attacking 24 separate sites. By the end of December, 52 sites had been bombed. The British thought that perhaps as many as 36 had been damaged, with 21 very badly damaged. Sadly, this proved not to be the case. The true picture was that only seven sites had been destroyed; 30 French civilians had been killed, with no German casualties whatsoever.

At this stage the Germans were still building ski sites faster than the Allies could destroy them; by mid-January they were completing two new sites every three days. However, by then the Allied heavy bombing was beginning to take effect. The damaged sites began to take too long to repair; more than half of the first hundred were simply abandoned, while efforts began to focus on finishing the new sites.

Meanwhile London and other cities, such as Bristol, Hull and Cardiff were under attack during the "Baby Blitz" (Operation Steinbock) between January and April/May 1944.

Originally the German V1 attacks had been due to start on 15 February 1944, but nothing happened. A month later on 17 March, Colonel Wachtel was assured that even by 15 April there would only be 3,000 flying bombs available in total. What should the strategy be, a heavy bombardment, or a continuous but lighter attack? By the end of March, 9 sites had been totally destroyed, 35 had been badly damaged, 29 partly damaged and 20 slightly damaged, a total of 93. Only 11 had escaped.

On 17 February, the Air Ministry issued a new directive, that the primary objective remained to destroy the German Air Force, but that neutralising threats under Crossbow remained a priority. There was a degree of concern that the Crossbow raids could detract from the preparations for the Normandy landings, but the raids continued at a high level. In December 1943 3,217 tons of bombs were dropped; in January the total rose to 6,726 tons and in February 5,532. In March it was 4,211. In April, with more daylight and better weather, the total rose to 7,248 tons. Meanwhile the factories producing flying bombs were regularly attacked.

Perhaps predictably, the Germans began to increase their defences round the ski sites; they brought in anti-aircraft guns and by the end of May they had 520 heavy guns and 730 lighter calibre guns. The defences round Cherbourg, where the ski sites were believed to be pointing towards Southampton, were also strengthened from 120 guns to 200.

So far, the Allies had already lost 154 aircraft and 771 of their aircrew were dead or missing. 462 of the men were from the US Eighth Air Force. By the end of May, 82 of the 96 ski sites were believed to have been put out of action, with the Americans playing a large part. Unfortunately, the French rural population were the ones who suffered the most, as the saturation bombing providing the most effective method of damaging ski sites, which were located in village or rural areas, also caused significant damage to buildings and their inhabitants.

The launch sites continued to be hit heavily, despite the increasing build up to D-Day. Between 5 December 1943 and 12 June 1944, almost 32,000 tons of bombs were dropped, most of which (23,000 tons) landed on the ski sites. Thanks to the Allies, most of these sites were never used.

Plans and training for air-launched flying bombs

There had been little information discovered about plans for air launches; understandably Allied intelligence had been concentrating on the ski sites as these had already been identified as part of an obvious threat. The air launch trials carried out over the Baltic off Peenemünde showed that the best carrier aircraft was the Heinkel 111, a heavy bomber. The Heinkel 111 had a crew of 5. This was made up of the pilot, a nose gunner who doubled as the bombardier and navigator, a dorsal gunner who operated the radio as well, a waist gunner, and a ventral machine gunner.

The Heinkel 111 had an average airspeed of about 360 mph. It required a minimum launch speed of 150 mph in order to carry the missile without stalling. The flying bomb could carry enough fuel to last about 5 ½ hours with a maximum expected flying time of about 4 hours. The research and development work took place at Usedom on the Baltic coast.

The air-launched flying bombs were suspended from a shallow pylon mounted under the widest part of the Heinkel wing root. This was as close as possible to the centre line of the aeroplane. The starboard wing was used in training and later in operational flights. Apparently, this handled sufficiently well, although once the bomb was loaded it went on to reduce the aircraft speed by about 20 mph. The flying bomb was detonated early in the launch by a spark plug, activated by a cable from a power supply in the Heinkel carrier plane. The air for mixing was provided by the forward thrust of the missile, initially under the wing of the Heinkel but later by its own forward thrust.

Early in 1944 the third Gruppe of the German bomber unit Kampfgeschwader 3 [III/KG3] was selected for air-launch training; it was then moved to Karlshagen airfield, Peenemünde. A group of Luftwaffe personnel who had previously done experimental work were chosen to train III/KG3 crews; they did a ten-day conversion course, involving three flights of one hour each. On 16 May 1944, Field Marshal Keitel issued a directive saying that the long-range bombardment should start in mid-June. The air-launched Heinkels should be part of the weapons to follow the initial attack. III/KG3 should operate out of these airports: Beauvais-Tillé, Parmain-l'Isle Adam and Roye-Amy.

The course was completed on 10 June, and the first III/KG3 crews were posted to airfields in northern France. The original idea was that they would join the start of the V1 campaign (as outlined in Field Marshal Keitel's directive of 16 May). However, it soon became obvious that they were not ready and thus unable to contribute at this stage. By sheer chance, the Allies had bombed the airfield at Beauvais/Tillé in mid-June, destroying a number of Heinkel 111s on the ground. The air-launched contingent would not in fact take part until early to mid-July, and it was not until the ground-based sites had been overrun that the He111 air launches came into their own. For now, this method was ignored in favour of the more traditional launch sites.

There were still restrictions on what could be reported about the new secret weapon. On 22 February 1944, Churchill mentioned in the House of Commons an "attack on this country either by pilotless aircraft, or possibly rockets, or both, on a considerable scale". The previous month, Herbert Morrison had met some carefully chosen newspaper editors to warn them about the V1. In February he wrote to the regional commissioners of the five civil defence regions to alert them: "The main threat is now from pilotless aircraft".

On 26 April, the alert was repeated in more detail. The regional commissioners were told that police, air raid wardens, and members of the Royal Observer Corps, based in areas likely to be affected should now be warned to prevent publication of any information that might reveal to the enemy where the missiles had fallen. These instructions went out to posts across most of southern England and included a description of the pilotless aircraft itself. It was described as resembling a small monoplane, with a wingspan of about 20 feet and a maximum speed of 400 mph; it was likely to be cruising at about 6,000 feet.

The Home Guard took this news very seriously, but as time went by and no attack materialised, there was a sense of optimism. Even the Air Ministry began to hope that by the end of April the remaining ski sites could be knocked out and all the concerns about flying bombs might disappear.

However, at the end of April 1944, one of the photo interpreters at Medmenham spotted something new and different: a long concrete platform with studs and a heavily camouflaged square building further away. This was near a village called Belhamelin, on the Cherbourg peninsula. It was a much simpler type of launch site, initially hard to spot, but within days twelve had been found. By 19 May, nineteen had been found. Nevertheless, the Allies largely ignored them; only one raid was made on the site, on 27 May, by Typhoon fighter-bombers. The modified sites were reduced to two elements: concrete foundations for the launching ramp and the square building where the V1 would have its compass set. In future the missiles were to be delivered already fuelled and then dispersed among the trees for camouflage.

On 11 May, a "radio bomber" or a "Nazi mystery plane" crashed in Sweden. The newspapers alleged that it was a "radio-directed flying bomb", a flying bomb with a pulse-jet engine. Analysis by RAE Farnborough confirmed it was aerodynamically feasible and further analysis agreed its guidance system, making reference to the square building on every launch site. The plan was to couple the attack with the beginning of the proposed invasion. On 16 May Hitler gave his final orders; the V1 attack on London was to start in the middle of June. Colonel Wachtel began to move his men from the ski sites on 20 May to the modified sites.

By the beginning of June more than sixty modified sites had been found, most of them oriented towards London. The day before D-Day Wing Commander Kendall came to a Crossbow meeting in London. He told them that the modified sites in France, along with perhaps some ski sites that they previously had thought to be abandoned, could be made ready for launch within a couple of days. The interpreters at Medmenham were very concerned; they realised the threat had been under-estimated, as Air Chief Marshall Hill later appreciated. During the first two weeks of June, the Germans were able to continue their preparations to plan their attacks, regardless of the Allied invasion. Neutralising the original ski sites had failed to prevent the danger, which remained imminent. 93 ski sites had sustained at least some damage; only 11 escaped completely.

It is poignant to read what happened in the months leading up to June 1944. The Allies were trying hard to destroy or disable V1 launch sites and weapons as soon as they were spotted, while the Germans continued to develop new ways of bringing the V1 project to fruition. Both sides were running out of time. The Allies were finalising their plans for the Normandy landings during the same period, and it was perhaps inevitable that these should take precedence. Vast numbers of troops were being marshalled in great secrecy along the South coast. Most people would have been aware that something momentous was under way, even if they were uncertain of its exact format, and might have realised that a new and potentially decisive stage in the war was about to start.

The Allied invasion was originally scheduled for 5 June but by 4 June conditions were unsuitable for a landing; high winds and heavy seas made it impossible to launch landing craft and low cloud would have prevented aircraft from finding their targets. A 24-hour delay until Tuesday 6 June was required, so that the weather could improve sufficiently for the landings. The invasion began shortly after midnight and the landings began at 06.30 on the 6th. One of the unexpected consequences for the Germans was that the Allied bombing raids that accompanied the landings wrought havoc with the French railway system; as a result, many of the catapults for the V1s failed to arrive, and the vital ingredient of permanganate of potash (required for the explosive mixture powering the V1) was in short supply. The start of the V1 operation was postponed yet again.

Meanwhile British intelligence noted that by 10 June there were wagons moving to France, along with hectic activity on modified sites. An attack was felt to be imminent… as indeed it proved. Dr Jones's suggestion that the attack would come at D-Day +7 was uncannily accurate. The interpreters at Medmenham had already been warned to be watchful and to stay alert, but further reconnaissance flights had to wait until after D-Day, and the next set of updating sorties did not take place until 11 June. Ten sites showed signs of considerable activity. In response, the Allies attacked three supply sites.

Ironically it was the success of the Normandy landings that made the start of the German V1 attacks unavoidable. The Germans had to go ahead with the V1 launches in an attempt to destroy British civilian morale. After all, what did Hitler have to lose at this stage? The V1s had been christened revenge weapons; now was the time for them to live up to their name.

There was yet another last-minute postponement. The start of the V1 operation, originally scheduled for 12 June, was put back again just before midnight that day. However, it was only put back by a matter of hours and was rescheduled to start on 13 June just after 03.30. It was a cold and overcast night. Soon after midnight the Germans began by firing about thirty heavy shells towards Folkestone, damaging property; they also fired towards Maidstone, further inland. These were intended to divert attention from the imminent arrival of the V1s. Just after 04.00 there was an air raid warning over most of Kent. It was followed by an all clear, then almost at once there was another warning.

The flying bomb campaign had begun.

Chapter 2

June 1944: The Doodlebug Summer Begins

The V1 flying bomb (known to the Germans as Vergeltungswaffe 1, Vengeance or Retaliation Weapon No 1) was a small jet-propelled aircraft, a type of early cruise missile. Its official name was Fi 103 (Fieseler 103), but V1 remains the standard description. In incident reports they were originally called PACs, an abbreviation of Pilotless Aircraft. The incident reports on the Guards' Chapel for 18 June referred to the V1 as a PAC, but the following day it was renamed a "flying bomb", and this more descriptive name persisted.

It had a number of other names and nicknames among the general public and the media. Hitler's 'secret weapons' became known variously as Divers, Buzz bombs, Robot bombs, Fly, Pilotless aircraft (or PACs), Flying bombs, Doodlebugs, Dingbats, Robots, Jet-Ships, P-Planes, Witches (many Polish airmen called them flying witches) and even Farting Furies or Farting Phillips. Perhaps doodlebug was the most common term among the general public; it was designed in part to minimise the terror and focus on the distinctive sound. It made a noise like a two-stroke motorcycle or "a strange continuous burping sound" while others likened it to the sound of a stick being drawn along a corrugated iron fence. (The unusual noise was because of the pulse jet engine.) But the flying bombs were dangerous, with thousands of civilians losing their lives to these weapons over the next nine months. Initially launched from the Pas de Calais, the V1s came in over the Channel at between 1,000 and 2,000 feet at speeds approaching 400 mph.

They proved a difficult target to intercept, much less to bring down and destroy.

The Germans initially referred to them as part of Operation Kirschkern (Cherry stone), the code name for the attack on London originally planned for 15 December 1943. Once that was postponed, the name changed to Maikäfer (Maybug) in May 1944; they were also known as "hell hounds" or "fire dragons" (the latter presumably because of the flame from the tail.) The V1 was a very effective weapon; it was cheap to manufacture as it consisted mainly of thin sheet steel and plywood. It also had no need for supplies of bombers, fighters or pilots to support its attack and its single use meant no need for repairs or extra personnel. It did not demand good weather or a "bomber's moon", nor did it need to be launched under cover of darkness. This had implications for civilian morale; the new attacks no longer came at night preceded by an air raid warning. The noise would start as a distant hum, then grow to a deafening noise. If you were lucky, you would hear it gradually diminish as the V1 continued on its way. More ominously, it might stop with no warning. The wait seemed interminable to the listener, but in reality it would last little more than twelve seconds – not long to try to find the nearest shelter. You might be able to shelter under a desk if at work or behind a wall or in a doorway if you were in the open, but there would not be enough time to seek a public shelter and probably not enough time to run from your home to your outdoor Anderson shelter, or anywhere else nearby.

There was also the element of surprise. Initially people would be drawn to their windows to watch this novel weapon; they even stood transfixed in the street, gazing up at the sky, paralysed by both fear and curiosity. What was it? And why had the engine noise stopped? This was why so many of the early casualties were caused by glass, with many facial injuries, especially eye damage.

How it worked

The original firing sequence was as follows:

At a modified site in northern France, the bomb was manhandled onto a modified four-wheeled trailer and put into position for firing. It then went to the checkout platform, where the wings were added and the warhead in the nose was armed. After that it moved onto the waiting platform for the final examination. It then went to a square non-magnetic building to correct and set the compass. (It had to be non-magnetic to avoid influencing the compass heading). The compass would keep the V1 travelling in the right direction, while the milometer (driven by a small propeller on the front) would check the number of miles already flown; the compass and the crude milometer would set the actual course of the V1, while a counter would set the number of miles to be flown. The gyroscopes were used to prevent the bomb over- or under-correcting correcting as it flew, controlling yaw and pitch so that it maintained its course.

Finally, it was fuelled and wheeled to the foot of the ramp (150 feet long and 16 feet high) where it rested on twin guide rails, with its tail separately supported on a sledge. Beneath the rails was a tube containing a piston that fitted into a metal housing beneath the bomb. The catapult was powered by burning hydrogen peroxide. As the pressure built up, the trolley was held back by a bolt, until this fractured and the trolley leapt forward, hurling the bomb into the air; the engine provided enough thrust to keep it airborne.

The V1 was made up of four sections: the main fuselage, a propulsion unit and two wings. (There is a V1 on display in the atrium of the Imperial War Museum, London, should you wish to examine one more closely.) It was just over 27 feet long including its engine; this was roughly the length of a wartime double-decker bus. Its wingspan was 17 ½ feet. Its overall weight was about 4750lb, about 1870lb of which was Amatol (a highly explosive mixture of TNT and ammonium nitrate, later Trialen). In front was a master compass to keep the aircraft on course. The course was pre-set beforehand; two servos could adjust the rudder at the tail or the elevators on the wings to correct any error. The height was controlled by an aneroid barometer, and the distance by a milometer, pre-set to a certain number of revolutions and operated by a small propeller. It started off at about 340 mph, then sped up as the fuel burned, reaching about 400 mph; it would cross the coast at about 2400 ft. It had a maximum range of about 150 miles, later increased to 250 miles to enable it to be launched from Holland or indeed Germany instead of northern France as the war progressed.

When the pre-set distance was reached, a circuit was closed which caused 2 detonators to be fired. These lowered two spoilers, which put the machine into a dive. As it tipped downwards, the fuel supply to the engine was cut off and so the engine noise would cease; this was the point where the light at the tail also cut out. About 12 seconds later the V1 would explode.

On the night of Tuesday 13 June 1944, between 03.30 and 04.00, the first ten flying bombs of the campaign were launched from France. Six of these failed; five crashed almost at once, while another vanished soon afterwards, presumably falling into the Channel. Of the remaining four, only one reached London.

It was still dark when, at 04.08, two men from the Observer Corps at Romney Marsh, Dymchurch, spotted "a strange shape, the size of a small fighter" in an overcast sky and making a noise like "a Model T Ford going up a hill". They instantly identified it from the description they had been given two months ago and telephoned Maidstone Observer Corps with the agreed code words "Diver! Diver! Diver!" Maidstone in turn relayed this to No. 11 Fighter Group at Uxbridge, who passed the report to Air Defence of Great Britain HQ at Stanmore. Whitehall was then notified; the long-awaited attack was finally under way.

The first flying bomb to land on British soil exploded at 04.13 at Swanscombe, near Gravesend. It fell on a field of greens and lettuces, leaving a shallow crater and badly damaging a house and a large area of crops. The noise it made was described as making cattle bellow with fear. The second landed at 04.20 in Sussex, near Cuckfield, narrowly missing a cottage near Mizbrooks Farm; Mrs Phyl Bowring was living there with her three young children and described "this sinister, eerie grunting noise", followed by "the uncanny silence when the engine cut out and then the ear-shattering explosion, and the house shaking and shuddering". The windows were blown out and all eighteen acres of the farm were "mown" by the blast; the whole crop was stripped to a uniform height. The fourth V1 crashed significantly later, at 05.06 in the garden of a large house at Platt, near Sevenoaks, killing a number of chickens and wrecking two rows of greenhouses. Initially it was thought that the shapes in the sky were enemy aircraft coming from France, distinguished by their illuminated cockpits.

The third was the only flying bomb of the four to reach London but did more damage than the other three put together. It exploded at 04.25 on the bridge over Grove Road, Bow. This carried the main line between Chelmsford and the LNER terminus at Liverpool Street. The V1 blocked all four lines over the bridge; it damaged a number of houses and there were casualties, some fatal. Six people were killed (their ages ranging from eight months to 55 years), the first of 6,200 such deaths that would be caused in the coming months. Thirty were injured, with ten people detained in hospital. 200 people were made homeless.

Initially there was the issue of deciding what had caused the blast. Was it a bomb or a crashed aircraft? By 06.15 the wreckage had been identified as a PAC (a pilotless aircraft) rather than a conventional bomb. Then there was a search for fragments, followed by the arrival of senior officials from the Ministry of Home Security to examine "it" in detail. There was a need to keep the attack secret from the Germans, so there was no reference to the raid in the morning papers. However, local and mainline railway tracks had been blocked, so thousands of people were aware a major incident had occurred. Their morning trains were diverted to Fenchurch St or stopped short at Stratford. Mainline services were affected as far away as Bishops Stortford and Cambridge, even though normal services were resumed by Friday evening of that week.

The official reaction was one of relief, as the attack had been far smaller and less significant than had been feared. Lord Cherwell remarked to Dr Jones that, "The mountain hath groaned and brought forth a mouse". The initial response was somewhat complacent; it was felt things could have been far worse. The existing defences were authorised to shoot down pilotless aircraft in heavily populated areas; this was quickly reconsidered once the implications became clear, and it was realised that this policy would mean that V1s would then be brought down directly onto their targets. As a result, the London guns were restricted and those under attack in London were aware of a depressing silence; it did not sound as if there was to be any attempt to retaliate, and the guns stayed mute.

There were many rumours, some attempting to explain the absence of a pilot. Had he ejected, or had he been blown to bits? Was it a German attempt to negotiate peace, or had it been a reconnaissance aircraft? Was it a failed invasion attempt? The flame from the tail was especially visible at night and gave rise to speculation; initially the number of pilotless aircraft sent over was exaggerated.

The War Cabinet felt that it was essential for the Germans to be denied information about the success of their attack. They "agreed that no public statement should be made about the new form of attack until the enemy had made it public or until the weight or extent of attack made a statement desirable...." (Longmate, *The Doodlebugs*, p. 99) They also decided that any future information published about air raids in the South of England would not give the exact location, referring only to "Southern England". The Home Secretary and Minister for Information agreed on this policy.

Unfortunately, it was already too late, as the Air Ministry had issued a communiqué which was published in the *Evening Standard* that afternoon and in *The Times* the following day. It mentioned that a "raider" had been brought down in the East End of London, and the wreckage had fallen across the LNER line. This meant that the Germans knew that at least one of their V1s had reached London. (The War Cabinet initially suggested there could be as many as 27 aircraft, coming in three waves, but later estimates dropped to eleven, not far from the actual number of V1s initially launched)

Over the next few days, the Germans worked hard to ensure that as many V1 sites as possible were fully equipped; fifty-three were made operational within the next two days. On 15 June Colonel Wachtel sent out new orders to his four subordinate commanders: "Open fire on Target 42 [London] with an all-catapult salvo" at 23.18, with a range of 130 miles, followed by sustained fire until 04.50 the next day, Friday 16 June.

This time the bombardment began promptly. By noon on 16 June, 244 V1s had been launched. There was the usual rate of attrition; forty-five crashed on take-off, destroying nine launch sites in the process and killing ten French civilians. Some of the rest went off course or simply disappeared, but seventy-three reached Greater London. Eleven were shot down over the capital; Flight Lieutenant Musgrave of 605 Squadron, flying a Mosquito, was the first pilot to shoot down a V1. No 3 Tempest Squadron, part of 150 Wing in Newchurch, Romney Marsh, were among the first to start to destroy the V1s; they shot down eight in the first day, and went on to score more than 300 kills.

This was the first many people knew about the flying bomb campaign. Although the V1 engine noise was distinctive ("a hideous racket", HE Bates described it), some eyewitnesses thought that the missiles were planes with their lights on, or aircraft on fire. They imagined that they were seeing enemy aircraft being shot down in flames, an encouraging prospect. Many of the missiles flew up the Thames Estuary and attempts were made to hit them as they rumbled overhead. The air raid warnings kept sounding, and some were still going off as people made their way to work in London on the Friday morning. In Hastings at West Hill, where St Clements Caves were used as an overnight shelter, people were concerned at the number of "aircraft" they could hear passing over. Normally they would have been told to move out at 09.00, but on this occasion they were told to stay put. Many people began to feel a strange sense of foreboding. Later that morning, staff at the Ministry of Supply in London were sent to the basement for safety and remained there for much of the day. Clearly the arrival of the V1s could be concealed from the public no longer.

Herbert Morrison made a statement in the House of Commons where he announced that a new weapon, pilotless aircraft, was now being used; a small number had been used on Tuesday 13 June and "a larger number was used last night and this morning". There was to be no information about where the raids had taken place, beyond a vague reference to "southern England". This was to ensure that the enemy did not know where their flying bombs had landed. He urged that everything possible should be done to minimise the attacks by obliterating the launch sites in France and hence removing the threat at source.

Air Marshal Sir Douglas Evill, Vice-Chief of the Air Staff, spoke of 150 "aircraft", 50 of which had fallen in Greater London area from about 40 sites in France. They flew at a height of between 1,000-4,000 feet, so were within range of light anti-aircraft fire or barrage balloons. Allegedly eleven had been shot down by fighters, twelve by anti-aircraft guns.

At 12.15 on 16 June Admiral Thomson, chief press censor, issued a confidential memorandum to the press which laid down stricter censorship rules than before. No information should be given about aircraft that had been shot down, "whether pilotless or piloted" so that the Germans would not be aware where the V1s were landing. Death notices in newspapers for those killed "by enemy action" (the traditional phrase, often seen on graves and indeed on death certificates) would now be limited to no more than three from the same district in any one issue. (This is why obituaries for those who died in the Guards' Chapel incident were couched in vague terms: "recently, in southern England" or "in June, by enemy action" both gave as much detail as could be permitted. A challenge for the contemporary researcher, as well as for the Germans in 1944.)

The BBC mentioned the new attacks on the one o'clock news that day, but their importance was played down. Many people were at work and missed the information. However, the evening papers made it the main story. The *Evening Standard*'s headline was "Morrison announces new German "air weapon": pilotless planes now raid Britain". Londoners travelling home that evening would have seen the billboards and become aware that the war had entered a new stage, even before they listened to the nine o'clock news or heard the distinctive sound of a V1 coming over.

In the afternoon the Prime Minister held a Staff Conference where it was agreed to take all possible steps to neutralise the launching sites, subject to the demands of the Battle for France, to redistribute gun, searchlight and balloon defences to counter the attacks, to avoid sounding an air raid warning for just one aircraft and to engage with pilotless aircraft.

Meanwhile a chance raid on 16 June on Beauvais-Tillé airfield in France by USAF destroyed 8 Heinkel carrier aeroplanes on the ground and delayed the start of the air launch programme.

That weekend was not only the first but also the worst for those experiencing the new weapons. The Ministry of Home Security issued new guidance: if you saw or heard a V1, you were to take cover at once. If the engine stopped or the tail light went out, an explosion was imminent, within 5 to 15 seconds. You should try to take cover from the blast and "use the most solid protection immediately available".

St Mary Abbot's Hospital, Marloes Road, in Kensington suffered a direct hit just after 04.00 on 17 June. Five nurses, six children and seven adult patients were killed, with 33 casualties transferred to

St George's Hospital, Hyde Park Corner. All the remaining patients were evacuated, and the hospital had to be closed, so that its 832 beds were no longer available for victims of subsequent V1 attacks. This was the first of no fewer than seven hospitals to be hit during the first week of the campaign.

By 06.00 on Saturday 17 June, just over 24 hours after the start of the attacks, fourteen London boroughs had been hit; eighteen people had been killed at St Mary Abbot's and almost 250 injured there and elsewhere. Later that day a V1 landed on a shopping centre near Clapham Junction, with twenty-four killed and twenty-five severely injured.

By 18 June the raids were becoming more frequent. It's easy to imagine that central London was the target but in fact outer London was also affected. A Teddington writer noted: "I've just realised that yesterday, 18th June at 07.30, back in 1944, was the day that the V1 'doodlebug' landed in Normansfield Farm and blasted in the front of my family home in Holmesdale Road. My Grandma was in bed in the downstairs front room and was lucky to just have cuts and bruises from the bricks, wood and glass. My Mum and her 3-year-old son were in the back room and were ok. According to my Mum's letter to my RAF Dad when they were evacuated, her mother suffered from shock for many months after that experience... and no wonder". The barn at the farm was completely demolished and there was a fire, along with blast damage to about 300 houses. Thirteen people were injured.

Guards' Chapel Sunday 18 June 1944

Westminster was hit by V1s for the first time on the morning of Sunday 18 June. It began when a V1 hit Hungerford railway bridge, demolishing one side of the tracks; this was approximately the five-hundredth V1 to reach London since the raids had begun, less than a week before. There was another attack at Carey Mansions in Rutherford Street, just before 09.00; ten people were killed and 62 others seriously injured when two blocks of flats were demolished. However, the third V1 was to cause far more destruction; it was described afterwards as the most serious V1 incident of the war.

The Guards' Chapel had been built in 1838 and was also known as the Royal Military Chapel, St James's Park. It formed part of Wellington Barracks, home to the Brigade of Guards. It had been attacked before during the Blitz of 1940, when all the windows had been blown out, with the pieces of glass sent for reconstruction. On 16 November 1940, a HE bomb hit the rear of the building and a shower of incendiaries landed on the Chapel roof. The whole roof was destroyed, with only the brick vaulting undamaged. The services moved for the next three weeks to Christ Church, Westminster. The roof was replaced with one made of concrete, which seemed eminently sensible and far less vulnerable to fire; sadly, it would later prove to have its own disadvantages. The Chapel re-opened for worship just before Christmas 1940.

The Guards' Chapel, Wellington Barracks, was an integral part of the Guards' lives. That Sunday was special: a mixed military and civilian congregation had gathered for morning worship. It was a bright and fairly warm day, sunny and pleasant to the extent that some of the Guards officers chose to spend the day at their boathouse at Maidenhead, instead of attending the service. With hindsight, that proved to be a wise decision.

The morning service was to commemorate Waterloo Day, a special day for the Guards and one that marked the defeat of Napoleon at the Battle of Waterloo on 18 June 1815. For many that day, it was also an opportunity for Guardsmen, their families and friends to give thanks for the success of the D-Day landings that had begun only 12 days before. The tide of the war in Europe was turning and people were eager to celebrate the occasion. Mothers, wives and daughters had all come to the Chapel to pray for their loved ones fighting overseas. The music at the Chapel was well-renowned and that day the Coldstream Guards' Band were playing, conducted by Major Windram. There were about 300 people, military and civilian, in the congregation. They included an American Colonel, an Australian padre, Stanley Baldwin's son-in-law and the sister of the painter Edward Le Bas, as well as a large number of Guardsmen. A number of nurses also attended wherever possible, with seats reserved for them when they were off duty. In many respects it was a microcosm of society.

Elisabeth Sheppard-Jones was serving in the ATS (Auxiliary Territorial Service) and had arranged to meet her childhood friend Pauline Gye (an air raid warden and hospital nurse) that morning; they had grown up together in Penarth and were now in London on war work: "As it was early and it was Sunday, a good way of sorting a long day would be at divine service at the Guards' Chapel, Wellington Barracks...a place loved by us both". They sat on a bench and watched the Guards drilling on the square before entering the Chapel and taking seats near the back.

The service began promptly at 11.00. The musicians of the Coldstream Guards were to play, while the Bishop of Maidstone (Dr Leslie Owen), was to be the guest speaker; he took a seat in the sanctuary, while the band played in the gallery. The new chaplain to the Brigade of Guards, the Reverend Ralph Whitrow, was officiating.

Lord Edward Hay (Commanding Officer, Westminster Garrison) read the first lesson and was walking back to his seat. A distant buzzing became the sound of an approaching V1 and the noise became a roar overhead. The congregation began to sing the *Te Deum*, just as the engine cut out.

Keith Lewis, a young Grenadier Guardsman, had been detailed to the choir. He described what came next:

> "It was during the reading of the lesson when it all happened. The Commanding Officer...was about halfway through the text when we heard the by now

familiar "motor-cycle-engine" sound of a V1. It became quite loud but I was sure it would continue on its way to some other unfortunate part of London, as all the others had done so far.

"Suddenly the engine noise stopped. What happened then was all within a nano of time, although I still see and hear it in sequence thus: a large semi-circular area at the top of the south wall collapsed; there was an intensive blue flash; I saw the Commanding Officer still standing but backwards at an angle of around 45 degrees. I remember noticing the ash-grey colour of his face (and later, I concluded that he was already dead at this moment); there was a very loud explosion (again later, I likened it to the loudness of a bang of an AA gun outside in St. James' Park); then some giant was hammering me all over my back."

Elisabeth Sheppard-Jones was towards the back of the chapel:

"Then there was a noise so loud it was as if all the waters and winds in the world had come together in a mighty conflict, and the Guards' Chapel collapsed upon us in a bellow of bricks and mortar.

"There was not time for panic…. One moment I was singing the *Te Deum*, and the next I lay in dust and blackness, aware of one thing only – that I had to go on breathing."

The choir had just begun the Sung Eucharist when the V1 nosedived onto the Chapel roof, exploding on impact. The direct hit completely destroyed the roof, most of the supporting walls and concrete pillars and the portico of the Chapel's western door. Tons of rubble fell onto the congregation, burying many of them to a depth of ten or twelve feet. Only the apse of the Chapel was left intact.

An initial City of Westminster ARP assessment put the number of casualties in the hundreds. 124 soldiers and civilians were killed then or afterwards, and 141 others were seriously injured. 102 were sent to hospital with serious injuries while 39 were treated at first aid posts. The Guards' Chapel incident was the most serious V1 attack of the war. It was a first and most graphic illustration of what a V1 could do in the first week of the flying bomb campaign.

Dr R.V. Jones (Churchill's principal scientific adviser tasked with countering the V-Weapons threat) and his colleague Charles Frank were at work that Sunday morning in the SIS(MI6) HQ offices at 54 Broadway. Soon after 11.00 Dr Jones was on the telephone to Bimbo Norman at Bletchley Park when he heard an approaching V1. Then the engine cut out. Dr Jones got under his desk to take shelter. There was a deafening explosion. Norman asked if they were all right and was assured that they were. Dr Jones then went out to see what had happened. He spoke of 30 seconds of silence, then the sound of people running into the street.

The bomb had fallen about 150 yards away on the Guards' Chapel. It killed over 120 of the congregation including many of the Coldstream Guards Band and their Director of Music, Major Windram. The high death toll included the officiating Chaplain, Reverend Ralph Whitrow, several senior British Army officers and a US Army Colonel.

Dr R.V. Jones recalled: "One lasting impression I had was that the whole of Birdcage Walk was a sea of fresh plane leaves, the trees had all been stripped and I could hardly see a speck of asphalt for hundreds of yards" (R.V. Jones: *Most Secret War; British Scientific Intelligence 1939-1945*').

"The Guards had everything under control and were already carrying out the dead. But that sight, coupled with the sea of fresh green leaves that had been torn from the plane trees in Birdcage Walk, brought home to me the difference between one ton of explosive in actuality and the one ton that we had predicted in the abstract six months before."

The Scots Guards had been drilling on the Square and were quick to help coordinate the rescue effort, while the WVS set up an incident inquiry post. As the clouds of dust subsided, first aid teams and heavy rescue crews arrived to find a scene of utter devastation. An initial City of Westminster ARP assessment put the number of casualties at 400-500. At first, the debris appeared impenetrable; the smashed remains of walls and the collapsed roof had trapped a large number of victims. The rescue services and Guardsmen from the Barracks immediately began freeing survivors from the wreckage and carrying them out. The doors to the Chapel were blocked; the only access point for the rescue teams lay behind the altar. Doctors and nurses were obliged to scramble in between the concrete walls to administer morphine and first aid. Several rescuers and survivors later recalled that the silver altar cross had been untouched by the blast and the candles continued to burn. The operation to free them all from the devastation took more than 48 hours; the last of the dead bodies was not recovered until the Tuesday evening.

The whole of the surrounding area was damaged by the blast. Even Buckingham Palace was affected and many of the windows there were broken. Many of the nearby mansion flat blocks, including Broadway Buildings and Queen Anne's Mansions in Petty France, also suffered blast damage, including one used by US news correspondent Walter Cronkite.

As the V1 campaign against London intensified, the Guards' Chapel attack received much publicity in the international press and was highlighted by journalists and in government statements as a particular atrocity. The Chapel itself was almost completely ruined. The rubble included the remnants of over two thousand small memorial plaques, dedicated to the service of Guardsmen since 1660. Despite the damage, part of the Chapel was re-opened for services in time for Christmas 1944. Today's Guards' Chapel was rebuilt on the same site during 1962-1963. Just inside the Chapel's west entrance, a large engraved wall memorial and book of remembrance record the soldiers and civilians who died in the 1944 attack. The original altar cross and six silver candlesticks still adorn the Chapel's altar.

There were many victims, too many to write about individually or in great detail, but the brief biographies below give some idea of the range of casualties, both military and civilian. The deaths involved a microcosm of society: some among the "great and the good", some career guardsmen and their families, others nurses on their day off. So many families torn apart by one incident on the first weekend of the V1 campaign.

Two young women, Edith Anne Farmer and Joan Ruth Duncan, were inseparable friends. They decided to join the Wrens (WRNS) together and had applied to serve abroad. They attended the Guards' Chapel service that day, died together, and were buried in the same grave in Romford Cemetery. (Edith Farmer's maternal grandparents, Emily and John Eustace East, died in another V1 incident at the King Henry VIII in Southwark on the evening of the following day, Monday 19 June – an example of the sheer randomness of the V1 death toll.)

Tony Titcombe had been a bookseller and had worked abroad before he joined the Coldstream Guards in 1940. He went overseas in January 1941 and served in the Western Desert Campaign. He was taken prisoner in June 1942 at Tobruk and was in prisoner of war camps in Italy until September 1943, when he managed to escape. He rejoined the lines after a thirty-day walk to freedom and returned to the UK on Christmas Eve, 1943. He had applied for leave to celebrate his wedding anniversary and young son's birthday on 20 June 1944, but this could not be granted; instead, he died in the Chapel.

The Mitchell family had planned to meet in London that weekend and attend the service. Janet Lockett Mitchell (British Red Cross Society) was nursing in London but had been granted 24 hours' leave, so she and her mother Vera (Women's Voluntary Service) decided to join her elder brother Lieutenant Michael Bradstock Alexander Mitchell at the Guards' Chapel service. Michael had joined the

Coldstream Guards in 1941 and was posted to 3rd Battalion. He was serving in Eastern Tunisia on 18 March 1943 when he and several colleagues were injured by a mine during an attack on the Mareth Line. His leg had to be amputated below the knee; his recovery was protracted, but by early 1944 he had been fitted with an artificial limb. He was able to return to duty that spring and was given the post of assistant regimental adjutant with effect from 18 March 1944. Exactly three months later he died with his sister and mother in the Guards' Chapel.

The musicians were playing in the gallery above the congregation when the V1 exploded. Several members of the Coldstream Guards' Band were killed, some by blast, others by falling masonry; another musician died of his injuries early in the following year. Over a dozen men were seriously injured and all the instruments were damaged beyond repair.

Major Windram, the Director of Music, had been suffering from angina and other health problems for some time; he was due to have a medical interview on 19 June, with the suggestion that 18 June would be his last day of active service. He was seriously injured in the Chapel and died on the operating table at St George's Hospital as they were about to amputate his leg. His wife had attended the service to see him conduct the band; she was badly injured in the attack and was too unwell to attend his funeral. it took her some months to recover from her injuries.

There were many others who died, including: two women on a telegraphers' training course from the Morse Training School; the American Colonel Gustav B Guenther, a friend of Eisenhower and a senior officer working in psychological warfare; Lieutenant Colonel "Ivan" Cobbold of the Scots Guards, latterly liaison officer with SHAEF; WO2 Nathaniel Turton, drill sergeant of the Grenadier Guards; elegant Society beauty, the former Gwen le Bas, and the wife of Lieutenant-Colonel William Gray Horton, Scots Guards; she attended the service as his representative; my mother's friends (she was revising for finals so had declined to attend the service): Beatrice Isabel Gardner, her cousin Margaret Ellen Norris and Marjory-Mary Gordon Souter, all from the YWCA Earls Court; several nurses, including Beryl Violet Clark (who could only be identified by the brooch in her hair); Sarah Louisa Courtney, widow of Thomas Courtney who had served with the Coldstream Guards 1892-1913; their eldest son Thomas was the Garrison Sergeant Major. Early on in the Blitz in October 1940, Thomas senior had been killed outright; his sixteen-year-old grandson Thomas had also died in that incident. Sarah's death at the Chapel meant that GSM Thomas Courtney had now lost both parents and his son to enemy action. Others included family groups, such as the Thorns: a mother, her younger son in the Royal Engineers and her American daughter-in-law who was in the WAAF. The military casualties were described as dying on active service; death in the Guards' Chapel on Waterloo Day is just as much "death in service" as on a field of battle overseas.

When I was researching the incident, I visited the City of Westminster Cemetery, Hanwell, to look at their records. There was one unidentified casualty, a woman who "died at the Guards' Chapel", according to the ledger of war dead, and was buried with the other civilian casualties on 29 June. So far I have been unable to identify her. I deduce she was a civilian as otherwise she would have been listed as one of the military dead and there is no record of her being in uniform. I am guessing that she attended the service alone as surely otherwise someone would have made enquiries; I have checked any leads from the WVS enquiry sheets, but to no avail. The vast majority of casualties were either military or civilians with links to the Guards. Until recently she was not counted as one of the dead from the incident; I should be most interested to have a name for her, or any other details.

It was late on the Tuesday evening, 20 June, before the last body was removed and the Chapel was cleared. Originally it was thought there could be several hundred casualties, a sign of the chaos after the explosion. The eventual total was 124 dead (65 military and 59 civilian casualties) either killed in the incident or dying soon after. There were 141 others seriously injured. 102 severely injured were taken to a range of London hospitals, including St George's and St Thomas', Westminster. As hospitals became overwhelmed by the sheer number of seriously injured, a request was made for all further urgent casualties to be directed to Brompton Hospital. (St Mary Abbot's had been closed to casualties after the V1 attack on it at 4 am on Saturday 17 June). 39 people less severely wounded were dealt with by first aid posts. As soon as some of the seriously injured were fit to travel they were moved out of London for safety; Major Windram's widow, for example, was moved to the Emergency Hospital, Old Windsor, where she remained for some months.

There were very few "walking wounded". The Bishop of Maidstone, who was to conduct the service, emerged apparently totally unhurt, although very shocked. He was sitting beneath a portico which sheltered him from the blast. (The portico now forms part of the rebuilt Chapel).

News of this awful tragedy was suppressed at the time because of censorship; nobody wanted the Germans to learn how successful the attack had been. It was early July before the news was released in the newspapers although rumours of the disaster soon spread across London. It was a graphic illustration of what a V1 could do, less than a week after the attacks had begun.

As the V1 campaign against London intensified, the Guards' Chapel attack received much publicity in the international press and was highlighted by journalists and in government statements as a particular atrocity. The Chapel itself was almost completely ruined. The rubble included the remnants of over two thousand small memorial plaques, dedicated to the service of Guardsmen since 1660; these formed part of the foundations of the new building. Despite the damage, part of the Chapel was re-opened for services in time for Christmas 1944.

Monday 19 June

By the end of the first weekend of the campaign, the casualties from V1 attacks had risen sharply to 499 killed, 2,051 seriously injured, 2,028 slightly injured and 633 wounded. In all, there had already been over five thousand casualties. 137,000 buildings had been damaged. This is an impressive total when you consider it was caused by 647 V1s in little more than four days of bombing; not all of them had even reached London.

That Monday, people were returning to work after the weekend. What were they anticipating? They would have seen the government warning about taking shelter once they heard the sound of a V1 coming over. Despite the embargo on identifying V1 incidents, anyone working in or near Whitehall would have been aware of the attack on the Guards' Chapel. It was a scene of devastation, with leaves blown off the trees, and broken windows in Queen Anne's Gate and Buckingham Gate. The rescue services continued to work through the night on Sunday and Monday nights; the last bodies from the incident were not recovered until late in the night of Tuesday 20 June. Many windows in other government buildings, such as the War Office, had been blown in yet again. The Civil Defence Committee met; they agreed that the guns in London would refrain from firing and decided that for morale reasons the new weapon would be renamed "flying bomb", rather than "pilotless aircraft". It was decided to discourage large gatherings.

At 17.00 the Prime Minister met with his advisers, followed by a Cabinet meeting. This endorsed all the earlier decisions from the Civil Defence Committee. By then the casualty figures had already grown to 5,856, with 526 deaths.

There were frequent air raid warnings throughout the day, and for many days to come. An official at the Air Ministry in Aldwych counted over thirty alerts in a single day; in the end most office workers resorted to ducking under their desks once the warning of imminent danger sounded. While the public had been told a little about the new weapons, they were yet to become fully aware of the threat, nor did they know what precautions they would need to take. Many people started to become hyper-vigilant.

A number of people died at their official posts that day: here are just two examples:

Bertha Massey Gleghorn, aged 33, was Britain's first woman police officer to die in the line of duty. She was killed by enemy action in London while on duty at Tottenham Court Road Police Station. She was just about to go back on duty when the rear of the station was hit by a V1 flying bomb. A brick wall collapsed and she was trapped in the rubble. A colleague remained with her, holding her hand until she could be released, but Bertha died in hospital later that day. Meanwhile at Brockley Road School, now the official HQ of the local Home Guard Company as the schoolchildren had been evacuated, five Home Guards from the 57th County of London Battalion were killed at about 22.00 when a V1 hit their post.

It is easy to imagine that the V1 attacks on London would be predominantly on central London, on well-known buildings (such as the Guards' Chapel), high-profile targets and ones where the civil defence services (heavy rescue service, ambulances etc.) were easily available and London's main hospitals were there to deal with casualties. This suggests that targets were carefully chosen and were all of strategic importance. The reality is that V1s were not especially accurate, particularly when contrasted with the bombings of the London Blitz of 1940/1941.

In particular, the number of attacks in suburbia is frequently under-estimated or simply ignored, partly because of the news blackouts at the time. While I cannot list all of them for reasons of space, I would like to offer some less widely known examples. I live in southwest London and during lockdown I took the opportunity to investigate some of the lesser-known V1 attacks in this area.

One shocking example is the six V1 attacks on Twickenham and Whitton on Monday 19 June within a 12-hour period. One can imagine the increasing sense of dread as people kept hearing the V1s coming over, relentlessly. The local residents would have been close enough to hear the explosions and to see the resulting plumes of dust. People were getting ready to start their week and were leaving for work. These were quiet areas near the river Thames in Southwest London; nobody was really expecting to see V1s quite that soon after the campaign started, nor was it felt likely that there would be repeat bombings in the same area, to the West of London.

The attacks began just after 07.00, with a direct hit on Whitton High Street that killed a married couple. The blast was felt as far away as Nelson School, which sustained damage to the front facing towards the High Street. Two more V1s fell some distance away without causing further casualties, but the fourth landed just before 08.00 in Twickenham, about a mile away, as people were having breakfast or getting ready to leave for work or school. It fell on the corner of Water Lane and the Embankment, by the river at Twickenham, then bounced a distance of more than 30 feet and entered Gotham Villas, a three-storey detached house. It exploded inside, killing six people instantly. These were a mother and her seven-year-old son, a 65-year-old man and his daughter and an elderly married couple, with four more people killed by blast at the riverside.

Freda Hammerton, the young daughter of one of the victims, described how: "On Sunday evening we could hear the V1s going overhead, then the engine stopping and the explosions and we began to realise that something very nasty indeed was happening.... The awful smell of dust and rubble everywhere – the muddle and the mess and the sheer misery." They spent the night in the Morrison shelter in the kitchen. Her father told her not to go to school that morning but asked her to stay in bed. He was a Thames pilot waterman; he had left to go to work at the local boatyard, but never arrived. He died in the incident that morning; he was only 36. Freda and her mother found his body lying by the riverside; he had been killed by the blast.

Twelve hours later, another V1 landed directly on top of "Tudor House" at the corner of Cross Deep and Holmes Road, Twickenham, not far along the river Thames from Water Lane; the impact cut the Morrison shelter at the rear of the building in half; it killed a mother and her four-month-old infant son as well as two passers-by and demolished a nearby pub, the Pope's Grotto. The final V1 fell in Longford Close, about a mile away to the southwest, killing a 76-year-old woman. In all seventeen people were killed that day in the Twickenham/Whitton area and many more were injured.

There were plenty of other V1 attacks during June as the flying bomb campaign began to establish itself. The events described here are just a sample of what happened during the first few weeks and are not intended as a comprehensive listing.

On the night of 22/23 June there was a random doodlebug attack at Ashworth Mansions in Maida Vale. A V1 hit a block of Queen Anne revival style mansion flats at about 02.30. It killed six or seven people and seriously injured 13. The dead included an elderly couple, their granddaughter, and an American citizen and violinist who was working for Claridges. Did they have time to take shelter?

On 23 June, there was the first successful attempt to "tip" a V1 flying bomb, using the wingtip of a Spitfire; 91 Squadron from West Malling was the first to develop this technique. The aim was to throw it onto its back so that it spun and crashed. It was an incredibly dangerous feat, but widely emulated. From now on, a range of defensive measures started to be developed, with Squadrons 91 and 96 leading the way.

The following night, 23/24 June, a V1 crashed near Petersfield, while another crashed at Marchwood, near Southampton. It became obvious that anywhere in southern England might be fair game; accuracy was not the major selling point of the V1s. While London was assumed to be the target, V1s could and did fall short. It would also soon become apparent that both Southampton and Portsmouth were becoming additional targets.

On 24 June there was an incident at Newlands Military Camp at Charing (near Lenham). The 6th (Guards) Tank Brigade Workshop (REME) suffered the Brigade's first casualties. At 06.18 a V1 was shot down by an RAF fighter and tragically crashed among the Nissen huts in the workshop area. There were heavy casualties. Out of 244 men, 46 REME soldiers were killed outright and 80 wounded. Six subsequently died of their wounds. The bomb also destroyed seven Nissen huts, the QM stores and an office hut; it damaged 14 vehicles and 16 motorcycles.

Brigadier Gough subsequently described the incident: "I heard a noise, looked up and saw a doodlebug coming towards us. It was being shot at from behind by a fighter-bomber. I started shouting, 'Take cover, take cover.' Then it hit the camp. The bomb struck the corner of a Nissen hut housing the soldiers…. For security reasons it was decreed that it should be an active service burial in a mass grave in the cemetery of the nearby village of Lenham. The grave was dug during the day by Scots, Grenadiers and Coldstream Guardsmen. At night, by lantern light, the burial took place. Each soldier was wrapped in their blanket, those who could be identified had a label attached, with their number, rank and name. The names were recorded and placed in a sealed bottle which was placed under a wooden cross."

Those killed amounted to about one third of the total REME soldiers stationed there. These had to be quickly replaced before the Brigade embarked for Normandy on 17 July. This event remains a significant event for those who served in the workshop and there is a memorial service every year on 24 June at Lenham Church, along with a service at the burial site on 11 November.

It is interesting to note that the tragedy was caused by an attempt to shoot down the doodlebug; clearly this tactic was already being used, less than ten days after the V1 campaign began. It had been agreed that V1s would not be shot down over London, whether by anti-aircraft guns or by individual aircraft, but there was no embargo on the areas outside. Gradually areas became designated "Doodlebug Alley"; those living between the coast and London became aware that the V1s tended to travel on specific routes. The flying bombs might fall short, but also they could be shot down. Either way those living under the flight path were at significant risk.

On the night of 25/26 June, Portsmouth had its first V1, with 19 minor casualties and 16 more serious in or near Locksway Road, Milton. There were no deaths. However, there would be another attack the following month. Norman Longmate stated, in his chapter "No sympathy for Southampton" in *The Doodlebugs*, that by 16 June 50 V1s were assumed to have been sent to Southampton, "although none had come down anywhere near it". On 26 June an experimental salvo of 12 or so V1s towards Southampton was ordered, but this was countermanded; Hitler ruled the following day that the sole target should be London. (Nevertheless, there were further attempts to attack Southampton and Portsmouth the following month.)

On the same night three V1s hit the Isle of Wight, near Newport. No fewer than 16 V1s flew over the island, with three crashing on the island itself. These may have been part of the V1 campaign for Portsmouth, or indeed Southampton; perhaps they ran out of fuel. The first flying bomb exploded in North Fairlee causing little damage and no casualties; the same was true of the one that landed at Duxmore. However, the third exploded near what is now the junction of Wellington Road and Carisbrooke Road, Newport. According to a Women's Voluntary Service report at the time, this one: "caused vast amount of damage to the houses and ... miraculously few casualties: only one death through blast and 14 persons needing First Aid attention."

There was one death recorded: a pedestrian, George Henry Woodmore, aged 51, manager at John Sheath of Upper St James's Street, Newport, who died on Carisbrooke Road. However, another victim, Emily Chiverton, housekeeper to Percy and George Long of 136 Carisbrooke Road, died on 27 June in St Mary's Hospital, having been taken there suffering from shock. (Percy Long died in August 1944, aged 62; his house had been damaged by enemy action and he had been obliged to move elsewhere. A further three residents of Carisbrooke Road died within the next few years, including Alfred Knight aged 68, of 139 Carisbrooke Road, who had been in poor health since his house had been wrecked by a flying bomb and who died in 1946.) So the overall death toll from the V1s may have been significantly more if you take later deaths into account. Several accounts of the bombings make it plain that people on the Isle of Wight found them terrifying, especially as these happened at night and entailed families spending the nights in air raid shelters.

Meanwhile the casualties were growing exponentially. By 29 June 1,679 people had died, 5,000 had been seriously injured and about 5,000 had been slightly injured. 270,000 houses had been damaged. By this stage the Government was issuing Morrison shelters to help protect people in flats and built-up areas, where they did not have garden space to install Anderson shelters.

On Friday 30 June 1944 there were many V1 incidents. I am proposing to examine five very different attacks to give a sense of the range of places and people involved.

The day began with the worst single V1 incident involving infant children. It happened in the early hours, at 03.37, at Crockham Hill, near Westerham. Little Mariners at Froghole, Crockham Hill, had been used as a home for evacuated children, but it was badly damaged by incendiaries, so they all moved to Weald House, on the edge of Crockham Hill Common. This had been chosen as an LCC (London County Council) "safe haven" children's temporary nursery for 30 small children, short stay evacuees from the London area. A staff of eleven women cared for the evacuees. It was in an isolated location and so was thought to be safe; it was less than a mile from the Prime Minister's country home at Chartwell. However, it suffered a direct hit from a V1 that had been hit by a fighter. The entire building collapsed. The young victims were all aged two years and under. Twenty-two of the thirty children died then or later in hospital, along with eight of the eleven nurses and domestic staff. Almost all the other inhabitants were seriously injured. The *News Chronicle* wrote: "One by one the tiny victims were recovered…. They were identified by the little labels tied to their ankles." Many had only just been evacuated there from London after their nursery school had been destroyed by incendiaries. It was several days before all the bodies were recovered and the task for local rescue personnel was particularly distressing because of the age of the children involved.

Later that morning at Otford, Kent, another V1 was shot down at 11.37. Joy Hilder (née Staples) was there with her sisters and wrote a vivid account:

"It started off as just another ordinary day – if you call any day during the Second World War ordinary. I was twelve years old, and on half-term holiday from the village school. My mother needed some things from the shops and sent me with my sisters, Doreen and Helen, and a friend, to the village.

…. "At the stone bridge we stopped, as we often did, to look into the river to see if anything new was swirling in the water…. We had only gone a few steps when, to our horror, the wailing of the air-raid siren echoed loud and clear across the valley. We immediately started to hurry, hoping to get home before any enemy aircraft appeared. But no such luck; the warning had hardly stopped when we heard the dreaded clattering sound of a doodlebug approaching fast. All our eyes were turned skywards, looking for the glimpse of where it would appear. Suddenly, from behind a cloud, the familiar shape of a Spitfire appeared at speed, and we heard the rat-tat-tat of machine-gun fire, repeated a few times.

"Silence followed. Still looking up I was thinking 'where is it?' Suddenly my friend and two sisters were running back towards me, crying, and I shouted to them to get down. Then I saw this large black object with one wing dangling loose spiralling down from the sky. There was a deafening explosion as it hit the ground in the meadow, just beyond the iron bridge and close to the river, sending up a huge fountain of riverbank earth and taking every leaf from the trees in the nearby apple orchard, which a few minutes later came floating down like pieces of confetti.

"I was knocked to the ground by the force of the blast and found myself in a crouched position against Mr. Roger's (Broughton Manor) wooden fence, which was falling apart. I got to my feet feeling very dazed and shocked to look for my sisters and friend. All I could see was broken telephone wires, earth and leaves scattered across the road, and I could hear someone screaming loudly. The odour of the river earth together with the stench of burning metal was overpowering. On taking a step forward, a large chunk of hot metal curled itself around my shoe, which I quickly managed to pull away. It was then that I noticed the blood pouring down my leg. Luckily, my two sisters were near me, and though crying, seemed unhurt. I asked them if they had a handkerchief to stop the blood, as mine had vanished with the shopping bag.

"Everywhere was chaos. An elderly man was sitting holding his head, his basket of strawberries scattered on the road. A girl from my school who had been walking just ahead of us with her dog, was lying injured in the road, crying.

"The barrage balloon men were the first to arrive on the scene, and I remember one of them lifting me over the tangle of wires and helping us along the road to the nearest house. A little further on were two ladies who had been hurt. They must have taken the full blast from the open field.

"We had been very lucky as we had been sheltered by the orchard which stood between us and where the bomb had fallen. The RAF men left us with Mrs Eggleton, who lived in the bungalow at the corner of Rye Lane. She told us to come in and sit down, even though her place was slightly damaged. She was very kind and bandaged my leg. Doreen had some small splinters in her face and hand but was not bleeding. My youngest sister, who was only four, was unhurt, but crying with shock. Our friend was injured in the foot and had lost her shoes.

"As we sat there recovering, my mother was seen running by, and Mrs Eggleton called out that we were with her. My mother could hardly believe we were safe. I'm sure she thought we were dead, and we were all crying together.

"A kind lady in a car took us to Sevenoaks hospital, where we were cleaned up and stitched. Enid Chalkin, a girl in my class, was also there. She was very distressed and crying for her dog, who had been killed. Sadly, she died from her wounds a few days later, after an operation.

"A couple of weeks later village children were evacuated to Devon for six months, returning after the flying bomb menace had ended, just before Christmas."

Ten others were injured by the bomb, six of them seriously. Just under 1,500 'Doodlebugs' fell in Kent during the V1 attacks, killing 152 and injuring 1,716 people.

About half an hour later there was an incident in central London, just after midday, when a V1 hit the staff annexe to the Regent Palace Hotel in Brewer Street, just off Soho. The hotel opened in 1914 and contained 1,028 rooms; it closed in 2006 and has since been largely demolished. The annexe contained 160 bedrooms for staff 'living in' (mainly maids). A chambermaid was killed on this occasion and a large number of people (168 in all) were injured in the surrounding streets. The building also contained a complete laundry service; bearing in mind that in the grand days of the hotel, there were over 1,000 people employed on the premises. The staff annexe building also contained a complete laundry service for all the Strand hotels in London.

The largest V1 attack of the five I am describing that day happened at lunchtime at the Aldwych. This is the semicircular street between

Kingsway, BBC Bush House, the Air Ministry Building (Adastral House), Australia House and the Waldorf Hotel; it is roughly due East from the Regent Palace Hotel, and links the Strand, Fleet Street and Kingsway.

At 14.07 the V1 glided over the Thames northwards towards Holborn, before exploding on the road between the Air Ministry and the northeast wing of Bush House, former home to the BBC External Services. It was lunchtime and a fine day, so people were taking advantage of the weather to go outside. They were queueing at the nearby post office, going to the bank, returning from their lunch break or travelling back to work along the Strand. Office workers were sunbathing on the roof of the Air Ministry's Adastral House, or looking out of their windows to see what was making that ominous sound.

When the V1 struck, the girls sunbathing on the roof were killed, and some of the workers were sucked out of their windows into the streets below by the blast. People in the streets outside were mown down and killed or injured by flying glass, while others died in the damaged double-decker buses that had been ripped apart in the incident.

Civil defence teams rushed to help the injured, cover up the dead and hose down the pavements. By coincidence, a fleet of army lorries was already parked nearby and these ferried the survivors to hospital with the help of 16 ambulances. A first aid post was set up in Bush House and the Women's Voluntary Service (WVS) dealt with hundreds of enquiries from those who feared family and friends might have been involved. In the Aldwych House first aid room, casualties were treated for the next three hours without a break.

More than 45 people were killed, possibly over fifty. I have been checking the casualty numbers and believe I have found a further five military dead, which would bring the death toll to over 50. They are:

Aircraftwoman 1st Class Maureen Savage, service number 2131098, aged 20, a teleprinter operator attached to RAF Leighton Buzzard, but temporarily attached to the Air Ministry, Bush House.

Aircraftman 2nd Class Murdo Macleod, service number 1572111, Royal Air Force Volunteer Reserve, aged 21, attached to the Air Ministry Unit.

Flight Lieutenant Douglas Hughes, MBE (awarded 1 January 1944), aged 30, service number 112154, Royal Air Force, attached to the Air Ministry. Both he and Murdo died in the same incident.

There were also two Australian airmen:

Flying Officer Dick Smith, service number 401713 of No 196 (Glider-Towing) Squadron, RAF, based at RAF Keevil. He was born in 1910 in Brighton, Victoria.

Flight Sergeant Oswald Edward Ferguson, BEM (British Empire Medal), service number 3913 of 10 SQN RAAF. He was a fitter and known as "Ossie". He was one of the key maintenance men of Australia's oldest Sunderland flying boat squadrons, of which he was an original member. His outstanding service had been recognised by the British Empire Medal; this was presented to his ten-year-old son Graham on his behalf the following year. "Ossie" was on sick leave at the time of his visit and he and Dick Smith were believed to have been visiting Australia House in the Aldwych or RAAF Overseas HQ in Kingsway at the time of the incident.

Almost 400 people were seriously injured and another 200 were able to go home after treatment: a total of 650 or more casualties from just one V1. There were many injuries from shattered plate glass, while one civilian was treated for a leg wound caused by a flying brass button. The foyer of the Aldwych Theatre was destroyed; an airman was killed at the box-office window as he was buying a ticket for that night's performance of "There Shall Be No Night". BBC Bush House was peppered with shrapnel; today, you can still see the blast damage to its façade. (It is now part of King's College campus.)

A former student was killed as she walked across the Aldwych to collect her degree certificate. (Iris) Nancy Rogers, BSc, aged 23, had been a student at Royal Holloway and Bedford College; she took her degree in June 1943 and passed with a second-class honours degree in Special Mathematics. On 30 June 1944 Nancy travelled up from her home in Southsea to collect her degree certificate. Sadly, she died at Bush House that lunchtime.

My mother, a final year languages student at King's, was sitting her degree examinations that June. The Great Hall on the Strand, with its huge windows, was being used as an examinations hall. All the students were aware of the risk from glass/blast. My mother was sitting her Latin paper. She remembered even many years later having to translate the phrase: "We who are about to die salute you" into Latin. All too accurate, just one evocative sentence to convey the start of that doodlebug summer.

As of 30 June, all concerts were cancelled because of the threat posed by the V1 bomb in central London. The Royal Albert Hall closed with immediate effect, and the Promenade concerts were suspended from July. Theatre attendances dropped; 25 theatres were still open in London at the end of June, but by 8 July the number had dropped to 17 and by 17 July only 8 remained open.

But there was one other significant incident on 30 June. Nobody had thought to cancel sports days.

The Training Battalion of the Welsh Guards had been planning to hold an athletics competition at the Metropolitan Police's Sports Ground, Imber Court at East Molesey on Wednesday, June 28, 1944, but bad weather was forecast. Instead the event was rescheduled for two days later: Friday 30 June.

The battalion was stationed at Sandown Park racecourse. Young soldiers completed their training there and waited for their posting; those who had been wounded convalesced before returning to operational duties. That Friday, the guardsmen and their instructors walked the two miles to Imber Court to take part in their sports day. It was soon after 14.15 and the second race was about to start. George Baker, who had just won the half mile, was walking along the track with the other competitors to the start of the next race, when the sound of a V1 was heard.

An eyewitness gave a vivid account of what happened next:

"The Welsh Guards were having their annual sports and fete down in Imber Court Park. This was a large sports ground with a large single storey stand on one side. I was sitting in the front row of the stand and to the left on the edge of the sports field the Regimental Band was playing a selection of music. Imber Court, Esher and Sandown Park were in what was then called "Doodlebug Alley." This day was no different to any other. We heard the familiar warbling sound of one coming over and looked up. Then its motor stopped and it headed straight for the stand in which I and many others were seated. A mad dash out of the stand and into the middle of the sports field. The band continued playing. Then the motor of the 'Doodlebug' restarted. Another look skywards. Now it was heading straight for the middle of the field. Abrupt about-turn and a headlong dash back for the stand. I dived beneath the first rows, helped on my way by the blast from the explosion. When I collected my senses and crawled out from below the stand I saw an unimaginable and truly horrific scene. The Doodlebug had landed smack on top of those of the band who had not managed to get out of the way of the bomb quick enough. Dead and badly wounded soldiers and WRAC lay all over the field. I believe 18 were killed and scores wounded that day. The scenes were too frightful to describe."

The bomb fell on the running track amidst those competitors walking towards the start of the hundred yards race, killing many soldiers instantly, including George Baker. The only runner to survive was Lieutenant Paget who suffered very serious leg injuries but survived after a two-hour operation. In all, 20 people died that day: 18 Welsh Guards, an army training officer and an ATS girl. About 100 people were injured. (The Welsh Guards had already suffered casualties earlier in the month when two guardsmen had been killed on 18 June by the V1 that hit the Guards' Chapel)

Five events in one day (and there would have been more). Approximately 102 deaths and about 780 injured. The figure for the injured would not include those who did not seek medical help at a first aid post or hospital, so would probably exclude those suffering from shock or cuts and bruises. Almost 900 casualties from just five flying bombs, in about twelve hours.

The doodlebug summer was well under way.

Chapter 3

July 1944: An Increasing Number of Flying Bombs

June had ended with the arrival of ever-larger numbers of flying bombs. As July began, the weather deteriorated, and the low cloud made it less easy to see the approaching V1s. Nevertheless, you could still hear them. People would stop what they were doing and wait, hoping that the doodlebug would continue its noisy flight. "Keep going, keep going" was the general sentiment.

Some groups were better able to sense that a doodlebug was coming. Cats and dogs would often take shelter even before the sirens went. There were many stories of animals having a sixth sense about approaching bombs. Families would watch their pet. If the cat or dog made for shelter the owner would be quick to follow. In reality, animals have exceptionally keen hearing and can register sounds too acute for human ears.

Apparently small children could also register higher frequency sounds. Presumably children had extra-sensitive hearing. A friend (Carole Tucker) told me that as a small child she could hear the doodlebugs coming some time before the air raid sirens went. When she was staying at her grandparents in Bromley, she could distinguish the noise of an approaching V1; she would then rush into the house calling out "Buzz bombs, buzz bombs". Then they would go to the underground shelter in the garden. This was dark and claustrophobic. She could no longer remember the sound the buzz bombs made though the memory of the sirens sounding stayed with her.

Evacuation

By the end of June, 231 children under sixteen had already been killed by flying bombs and 493 had been seriously injured. Although as late as 27 June the Cabinet had decided against an official evacuation scheme, by 1 July there had been a change of heart and a voluntary evacuation scheme was set up. The LCC (London County Council) began to register mothers with young families and children of school age who wanted to be sent away. They acted swiftly and on 3 July the first parties of evacuees were despatched. They went to the Midlands, the North, Scotland, Wales and the West Country; all places felt to be out of the range of the doodlebugs. On 6 July Churchill mentioned in the Commons that people were being sent away and suggested that non-essential people might wish to go.

Despite the memories of the 1939 evacuation, once again people were increasingly keen to escape the threat of bombing. All the parents who had been reluctant to send their children away in 1939 were being confronted with that dilemma once again, almost five years later. My grandmother knew that her only son was now working as a scientific civil servant near Bournemouth, just out of range of the doodlebugs; however, she and her husband were running a business in Acton, within sight and sound of the flying bombs reaching London. She told me that during the war she began to smoke cigarettes to deal with the stress. Grandma and Grandpa had a Morrison shelter in their scullery but I'm not sure how much reassurance it gave them.

Perhaps the situation felt different from that of autumn 1939. By now Londoners had more experience of bombing and sleepless nights. For many families, the father of the family was now away from home, in the services, maybe even fighting abroad. This left the mother and children, plus possibly grandparents sharing the family home. Did they want to stay in London? Would you send your children away, as others had done in 1939? Or would you go with them and try to get away from the Southeast? (Someone I spoke to said they had been evacuated a total of four times during the war and had been too young to realise why.)

Organising an evacuation scheme in less than 2 weeks (if you count 16 June as the beginning) and arranging for about 700,000 people to leave London within a month was an impressively swift response. That number would double before the end of the summer. Clearly the V1s were making life very unpleasant; London and the Southeast were starting to empty. There was a suggestion of an atmosphere of panic at Waterloo as people struggled to leave London. By 17 July 170,000 people had left, along with 530,000 private evacuees. After that the numbers rose sharply. (By the end of July, 7,000 women and children had left from the Borough of Twickenham alone). By 3 August 225,000 mothers and children had gone. Between 5 July and 7 September, 307,000 mothers and children had gone in organised parties along with 140,000 expectant mothers and 520,000 "aided" others. Eventually this figure would rise to 1.45 million, possibly even more.

Joy Hilder's account of an Otford V1 added, almost as an afterthought, "a couple of weeks later the village children were evacuated to Devon for six months, returning after the flying bomb menace had ended, just before Christmas." (This would have been in mid-July).

There was an unusual precedent for this. It was not just women and children who were evacuated. A rare breed of sheep had been sent away earlier in the war. In 1939 there were about 200,000 Romney sheep on Romney Marsh. In May 1940 the Marsh had to be fortified and partially flooded to protect the coast from invasion. The sheep had to be sheared and then sent away to hill farmers in Yorkshire; many were evacuated by train, others by road.

For those people who did not want to leave London, or were unable to do so, many took to sleeping in the Tube at night. About 73,000 people went there every night during the first two weeks of the flying bombs, though by 9 August only half that number were still going. Four new deep bombproof shelters opened in mid-July while Chislehurst Caves continued to be used, as were the caves in Hastings and Ramsgate Tunnels.

By now the combined defences of fighters, guns and barrage balloons had managed a kill rate of 40 percent of all the V1s launched, a huge improvement on mid-June but still not much of a comfort to Londoners who were having to face the new Blitz. While it was encouraging to know that the Allies were making inroads in Normandy it did not cancel out the fears of those who remained in a London that was being bombed by night and day. South London was getting the lion's share of doodlebugs, while the area between the coast and London, known as Doodlebug Alley, was frequently hit by V1s that fell short or were shot down. After all the kill rate still left a potential 60% of doodlebugs to be accounted for; while some would fail to launch and others would fall into the sea, a sizeable percentage remained.

The first week of July was the worst week of the flying bomb campaign. More than 800 V1s were launched in the first seven days. While not all reached London, a significant number hit Kent en route. "A flying bomb will often take somebody's life – in order to save London", commented Alderman E. S. Oak-Rhind, Chairman of Kent's Civil Defence Committee. While the capital got the worst of flying bombs, people in the southern counties had the peculiarly unpleasant knowledge that they might be killed by their own side.

H. E. Bates said it was terrifying for everyone in Doodlebug Alley; they had the chance to see and hear almost everything a flying bomb might do. At night it was even worse as you would just be listening and could not see what was happening. There might be a low-level roar that could be heard from 30 miles away; there could even be several at once, running in parallel. The worst sound of all was silence…as that meant the engine had stopped.

On 1 July there were yet more V1 flying bomb attacks on London on a range of places: Brixton, Upper Norwood and Gipsy Hill and

Bermondsey. A total of 61 people in South London perished during the day. Another hospital was hit, this time at Colindale, Hendon; the V1 demolished two ward blocks, and killed ten people. (Some had been injured prior to the raid.) Later that afternoon a V1 overshot London and hit the chimney of a Windsor Corporation Refuse destructor in Kentons Lane; it came down on houses nearby and seriously injured more than 250 people. Everywhere was covered in red dust.

The next day the assault continued, extending not only to London but also in varying degrees to all the south-eastern counties of the United Kingdom. A hundred and sixty-one V1s crossed the coast that day; some came down in Kent, but many got through to London. 30 more people died overnight, and a lot of property was damaged. One bomb hit a US Army camp, killing two soldiers.

On 3 July at 02.51 at Marden a flying bomb was shot down by AA fire; it fell on an Army camp in Pattenden Lane. Ten members of the Royal Army Service Corps and one of the Army Catering Corps were killed; they are buried in two collective graves in Marden Cemetery. There were eight serious injuries.

Allied fighter aircraft were starting to discover how to dive onto the flying bombs so that they could shoot them down. The bombs were faster than all but the latest Spitfires and Tempests so that the pilots had to dive from a height to gain sufficient speed to attack. Meanwhile many anti-aircraft guns were moved to the coast so that they could attack the V1s passing overhead.

On 3 July at 07.47 there was a major incident when a V1 bomb came down in Sloane Court East in Chelsea. (The recorded death toll varies because of wartime censorship and the sheer scale of the incident.) It killed at least 65 American servicemen, possibly as many as 74, who had been billeted in the area. Many of them belonged to the U.S. Army's 130th Chemical Processing Company, sent to the UK to assist with preparations for dealing with possible chemical warfare. The men had just finished breakfast and were preparing to board trucks for work. Suddenly a V1 appeared. The company commander spotted it and shouted "Buzz bomb! Buzz bomb!" Men dashed for cover, but those already seated in the truck had no chance to escape. The blast blew the truck into the side of a building, killing all inside.

Perhaps as many as nine civilians died, including a female air raid warden. At least 50 American servicemen were seriously injured. Members of SHAEF (Supreme Headquarters Allied Expeditionary Force) were also stationed at Sloane Court; two were killed and 19 were injured. There were possibly also casualties among the Women's Army Corps. It was felt to be the worst V1 incident affecting American troops. Some accounts suggest it was the second worst V1 incident of the war, perhaps if you rank it in terms of numbers of dead; the Guards' Chapel incident on 18 June had 124 deaths. Glenn Miller and his band had a lucky escape; they had been stationed at Sloane Court, but they moved the day before the bomb.

This was the first day during the V1 campaign that a Metropolitan police horse gained an award for bravery. Olga was a bay mare; she was used for crowd control and rescue operations near Tooting. On 3 July 1944, Olga and her rider PC J. E. Thwaites were patrolling Besley Street SW16 near the railway line when a bomb exploded 300 feet (91 m) in front of them. The explosion destroyed four houses, killed four people and caused a plate glass window to fall directly in front of Olga. Startled, the mare initially ran a short distance away from the blast until Thwaites was able to calm her and guide her back to the area. She soon settled down and allowed her rider to give help to survivors and divert sightseers away from the area. She was honoured for courage during active duty.

Later that day, air-launched flying bombs began to be used when III/KG3 began an attack on London. 14 Heinkels carrying V1s left Gilze-Rijen at 22.00; they headed for the Dutch coast and then changed to low-level flight over the sea to avoid detection by British radar. They climbed in order to launch their weapons; once the V1s separated from their Heinkels, the latter made a sharp turn and returned to base.

On the following night of 4/5 July, no fewer than 22 Heinkel bombers flew sorties during the night and launched V1 flying bombs from the air; they left Gilze-Rijen soon after 22.00 and all the aircraft returned safely. The bombs fell in south London in places such as Deptford, Streatham, Brixton, West Norwood and West Dulwich, killing more than fifteen residents and causing considerable damage to property. It seemed that the air-launched V1s had a different pattern of damage; they often glided down in a shallow dive and blew up on the ground. This tended to destroy houses and take the roofs off others.

Meanwhile, that night, the largest underground V1 storage site at St Leu was attacked with a number of 12,000lb (Tallboy) bombs dropped by 617 Squadron, led by Wing Commander Leonard Cheshire. These blocked the main tunnel and made the approach road impassable, as well as severely damaging the railway. After that, the average number of flying bombs launched against London dropped from 100 a day to less than 70, which in turn helped to improve the success rate against the V1s from 40% to over 50%.

Mid-evening on 5 July, another V1 hit southwest London. This time a flying bomb hit Teddington Film Studios on Broom Road, Teddington. It had been one of the few British Film studios to remain in action during World War Two and had been responsible for ten percent of Britain's film production. The bomb hit a large tank full of diesel oil; the oil scattered and ignited, setting fire to the stage, the office block opposite and other buildings. It completely gutted the main studio and killed "Doc" Salomon, the studio's American production manager, and two other staff. The Ministry of Works would not allow the material or labour to repair the damage and so the studios closed in October 1944. (The oil from the incident flowed down the Thames and poisoned a large number of fish, which were visible near Richmond Bridge for some days.)

By now the RAF were becoming increasingly skilled at shooting down V1s and the aerial assault was intensifying. The method of flying alongside a V1, getting one wingtip under its wing and tipping it, started to be developed; this affected the gyroscope so that the V1 crashed.

Nevertheless, the psychological impact these missiles had on the local population was devastating and by now the evacuation programme was well under way. People spoke of the distinctive sights and sounds that summer: the smell of fresh sap as the blast stripped bark and leaves from the trees, the smell of powdered brickwork, the sound of newly shattered glass crunching underfoot and the half-bombed houses and flats lying open to the gaze as you walked past. While these incidents did not appear in the newspapers, for obvious reasons, anyone walking through London would have been well aware of the damage.

On the night of 5/6 July V1s fell near Portsmouth and Lee-on-Solent and near Lake on the Isle of Wight, where one person was killed, at about 02.40. These are believed to have been air launched.

On Thursday 6 July, the Prime Minister made a statement in the House. He said:

> "Up to 6 am today 2,752 people have been killed by flying bombs and about 8,000 have been injured and detained in hospital. The number of flying bombs launched up to 6 am today was 2,754."

> He went on to say that between 100 and 150 flying bombs were being launched daily. Penicillin, previously only available to the military, would now be given to flying bomb casualties. He stated that a very high proportion of the casualties had occurred within London. He stressed that the priority had to be battle operations in Normandy and attacks on specific targets in Germany; "they come first".

At 02.35 on 7 July, another eight air-launched V1s were despatched against England from III/KG3's temporary base at Rosières, France.

The Heinkels returned successfully but two aircraft had collided on the runway prior to take-off. Most of the bombs were shot down, mainly over the Channel, but one got through and landed in Southampton.

The Germans now decided to drop the original name of "flying bomb" in favour of V1 (revenge weapon no. 1); it was intended as a direct reprisal weapon for attacks on German cities, with hints of worse to come.

On 8 and 9 July, V1s continued to hit London and cause casualties. On 9 July at 21.41 a V1 made a direct hit on the South Metropolitan Gas Company's gasholder in Kennington. There was a huge explosion and considerable damage to local houses. On 9 July the first deep shelter was opened at Stockwell; it was 130 feet below ground and held 4,000 people during its first night. A second deep shelter opened four days later.

The V1s of 9 and 10 July may well have been air launches as they could not be traced back to any launch sites in the area.

The following day, 10 July, the Heinkel bombers of III/KG3 resumed their attack and there were 30 sorties, with some crews flying twice. Seven V1s were shot down by AA fire, three by night fighters. A V1 fell in Battersea at 02.42, swiftly followed by a V1 landing in Clapham Road opposite Clapham North underground station at 02.55; both incidents caused deaths and damage to property. On 10 July in Penge a V1 hit a public air raid shelter, causing more than 100 casualties. Seven died at the scene, with a further two in hospital the next day and another nine on 12 July. Norfolk had its first V1, presumably by accident and possibly an air launch.

That night there was another attempt to attack Southampton. 22 V1s crossed the coast, but ten were brought down by night fighters and AA fire and all missed their target. The remainder fell wide, mainly in the New Forest (including Beaulieu and Brockenhurst) and around Southampton and the Isle of Wight.

On the following night, July 11/12, a further 29 V1s fell in Hampshire, all air-launched.

Just before midnight, 18 Heinkels set off from Rosières. A number of V1s crossed the coast, but ten were brought down by night fighters and AA fire and almost all missed their targets; only two hit Southampton, in Bitterne and Sholing. As before, the remainder fell mainly in the New Forest and around Southampton and the Isle of Wight.

At 01.00 on Wednesday 12 July, a V1 hit Swanmore Avenue, Sholing, Southampton, and is believed to have killed three people. Brian Martin, who lived on that road, told the story of how he, his younger brother Ray and his mother Doreen were already in their garden Anderson shelter; they went there every night as a matter of routine. The bomb actually landed in an orchard which backed onto their garden but the crater it made came right up to where their shelter was placed. There was a massive explosion, which destroyed a dozen houses. Brian thought they had been saved because of a blast wall outside the shelter door that their grandfather had built the day before, but there was one casualty: his budgie, which was later found dead, presumably from the blast. Another V1 injured nine people in Bitterne that night. There were two more V1s close by: one in West Wellow, with no damage or injury, and another at HMS Cricket (Manor Farm in Bursledon) where two naval cadets were killed.

More Morrison shelters were distributed in Kent from 11 July onwards; it was becoming apparent that the area was increasingly subject to attack, either when V1s fell short or when they were shot down. These were the indoor "table" shelters, designed to protect the inhabitants from blast. They had first been introduced in 1941 and were particularly useful to those without a garden. In July there were V1s every day; 50% of these landing in the SE Civil Defence region landed in Kent, 40% in Sussex, 10% in Surrey.

East Grinstead's worst V1 day came on 12 July when one was shot down over the town at 07.25 and crashed into the rubble of an earlier bombing raid on London Road from the previous year. This time three were killed and 41 injured with more than 400 homes, shops and offices damaged by the blast. The death toll was comparatively light because it was so early in the day. Within a few hours, the King and Queen visited the scene as they were in the area that day.

Later that morning, at 08.57, a V1 scored a direct hit on Beechmont, a large house near Sevenoaks, formerly the home of the Lambarde family. It completely destroyed the house, which was being used as an ATS (Auxiliary Territorial Service) base for the women who were maintaining the military vehicles stationed at Knole Park. Most of the women had already left for work, but two ATS privates (Grace Potter and Violet Calderwood) were killed and 44 injured. (The CWGC suggests it was 14 July, with three ATS girls and an officer killed).

Air Marshal Roderic Hill held a meeting to discuss the best strategy for the Royal Air Force and the anti-aircraft batteries to adopt to deal with incoming V1s. By the start of the month, it had become obvious that the gunners, airmen and balloon crews were so frequently getting in each other's way that a change of strategy was essential.

From 13 July, the gun batteries were to be redeployed to the coast, while the balloon barrage was increased by the end of the month. They decided to create two distinct areas reserved for fighters alone: one over the sea in front of the gun belt and the other inland behind it. Within five days, the guns were moved to between St Margaret's Bay and Cuckmere Haven, with 376 heavy and 572 light guns, among others.

This was partly because the gun batteries along the coast were to be given secret radio proximity fused shells; these could pose just as much a threat to nearby friendly aircraft as to the V1s. The system quickly justified itself; the gunners shot down 17% of all flying bombs in the area within a week. By the second week, the total was 24%, and by the end of August it was 74%. General Pile said he felt this gave more chances of bringing the flying bombs harmlessly down into the sea.

The government announced that up to 06.00 on 14 July a total of 3,526 flying bombs had been launched. However, since the night of 10/11 July no further night attacks had been directed at London. Nevertheless about 15,000 people a day were now leaving the city on packed trains; the mass evacuations were later thought to have saved many lives.

Air launches against Southampton and Portsmouth

During the night of 14/15 July, Heinkel aircraft of III/KG3 flew 23 sorties to launch V1 bombs against Southampton. Most were either abortive launches, missed or were shot down by night fighters; some hit the Isle of Wight. However, 13 hit the mainland and three caused heavy casualties. They were all apparently aimed at Southampton but in fact only one hit the city, the remainder being scattered far and wide with one landing as far away as Winchester.

The most serious incident was when a (presumably air-launched) V1 came down on Newcomen Road, Stamshaw in Portsmouth, at about 01.00. It was said to be heading for the naval base on Whale Island when the anti-aircraft guns on the Island shot it down; it crashed ten feet away from the back of number 89 Newcomen Road, killing 15 people and injuring many more, possibly as many as 98. The raid report described "very extensive house damage" in this and four adjacent parallel roads. The damage could have been still worse; all four roads ran down to a wide river creek at their western end, and this may have absorbed some of the blast. Numbers 83-93 Newcomen Road were destroyed along with two surface air raid shelters and there was heavy to moderate damage to 185 properties.

Frank Morris Channon (1881-1944) and Maud Mary Channon (1879-1944) lived at number 91, along with their son Frank Norman Channon (1904-1944.) Frank senior was a retired policeman. Another son, Frank Redvers Channon (1906-1944), lived at number 85, a few doors away. Frances Turner (1887-1944) was next door to Frank and her nephew Frankie (1937-1944) was staying with her that night. Charles Hills (1900-1944), his wife Ivy Agnes (1901-1944) and their sixteen-year-old son Malcolm were at number 89. Arthur (1910-1944) and Lilian Towle (1911-1944) were at number 86 across the road; they were celebrating their thirteenth wedding anniversary. All were killed outright. A thirteen-year-old daughter at number 83 died of her injuries in hospital later that day. Four further people died in Winstanley Road: a mother and daughter, a thirteen-week-old baby and a woman who could only be identified by her wedding ring. The woman's husband was left with such severe head injuries that he remained in hospital for the rest of his life; he died in 1953. Just one V1, but so much devastation; so much for the allegation that each V1 might perhaps kill one person. One of the children who died was a pupil at Stamshaw School, a few streets away. His fellow pupils had a collection in his memory and the school bought a framed picture of Christ knocking at the door. It was mounted in the main hall of the school, with a candle that was always alight, for the four children who had died in the incident.

Another air-launched V1 that night also had heavy casualties when it hit the village of Goodworth Clatford, near Andover, at 01.05, only five minutes later. It hit a telegraph pole and crashed into the village centre, killing six people. The Royal Oak and the village school were both destroyed in the attack. Three of the casualties were local residents. The other three, the Jones family, had come there from London the previous day. The husband and wife and their 17-month-old son had chosen the village because the husband had a few days' holiday, and they wanted a rest from the relentless bombing at Thornton Heath where they lived. Since the start of July, their area of London had suffered no fewer than ten attacks from V1s between 1 and 5 July, with a total of 42 deaths, followed by another two on 11 and 12 July, this time with 13 deaths in total. This represented a total of 55 deaths in under two weeks and within quite a small area.

Understandably they wished to escape from London, but it is tragic that they did not even survive their first night away.

A third V1 injured six more people, this time at Sholing, Southampton.

Air launch tactics

During the month the V1 strategy changed. The V1 operations from French airfields came to an abrupt end after 15 July when the Allied troops began to break out of Normandy. It was now time for the Germans to move to airfields better placed to evade the AA gunbelt in southeast England; in other words move east and north from France and withdraw to Holland. III/KG3 chose Venlo and Gilze-Rijen as their main air-launch bases. They adopted a low level approach to conceal their Heinkels from British coastal radar. They flew as low as possible, with heights of 300 metres over the coast, dropping to 100 metres over the sea, and with a flying speed of 170 mph. When approaching the launch zone, the aircraft climbed to 500 or 600 metres and its speed fell to 110 mph. Once the Heinkel levelled out, its speed built up once more to 170 mph or more, because the stalling speed of the V1 itself was 150 mph. The Heinkel aligned itself to the V1 course setting already chosen (which was also that preset before take-off in the directional compass of the missile). The automatic pilot of the flying bomb was started by the crew of the He111 while airborne. The Argus ramjet of the V1 started up and this was allowed to run for ten seconds before the V1 was released. (Those in the aircraft could tell the release had occurred because they could no longer feel the vibration from the V1 engine; they could also feel the Heinkel lift as the weight of the flying bomb fell away.)

During the startup period for the jet and for the ten seconds before the missile was released, the Heinkel was lit up like a beacon. Hans Hoehler, an aircrew member, memorably described the process as like "sitting in a lighted bus for all to see". The Heinkel crew felt very vulnerable to attack by night fighters and were anxious to return to base as soon as possible. The advice was to follow the missile for a short distance, then drop back and lose height to 100 metres to evade night fighter crews. The flights over the sea were only short; they were usually parallel to the Dutch and Belgian coast and there were flashing marker beacons for the duration of the operation. This made navigation relatively easy.

By 31 July British Intelligence sources had become aware of the new air-launch tactics; they had traced flying bombs being launched from the areas between Ostend and the Dutch islands from as early as 9/10 July. The launches had increased in scale from 18/19 July and at least nine sets of launches had taken place. They estimated 131 V1s had been fired from that area at night, between 23.30 and 04.00.

Allied pilots were becoming nervous about the devastating effects of the bombs they shot down, as these exploded on populated areas en route to London; however, the Air Ministry put the defence of London as a priority. This was an understandable view, but the V1s affected morale not only among those who were attacked by them, but also among those who were tasked with trying to circumvent the attacks. It was a cold grey summer, where the doodlebugs appeared and disappeared between the clouds. The smells of brick dust and plaster were all around in the suburbs, as well as central London. That summer you could also smell the crushed leaves from the trees after the blast. (Several people remarked on the smell of the plane tree leaves in Birdcage Walk after the Guards' Chapel V1.) Doodlebugs came over by day and night; sometimes they appeared to be travelling in convoys. You would hear the distinctive sound of the engines coming nearer, then hold your breath, praying that the noise would continue rather than stop abruptly. People were on edge. Although you tried to go about your daily routine, the constant "noises off" and delays to transport took their toll. You were never sure whether you would reach work, let alone return to your home and see your loved ones again. Families made sure they said their goodbyes, "just in case".

On Sunday 16 July at 16.40 a V1 hit Hastings at Hollington. It is thought that a US pilot had tipped the wing of the doodlebug. Sadly, it fell on a council estate, killing three and seriously injuring 47. One account mentioned "Our pet canary had been making a strange warning call all day." (Clifford de Meza, BBC People's War, https://www.bbc.co.uk/history/ww2peopleswar/stories/84/a4396584.shtml)

Monday 17 July saw a number of flying bomb incidents. There was a major incident in Suffield Road, Walworth at 05.13; 17 people were killed, and 150 homes were damaged by blast. Just over an hour later, at 06.28, it was the turn of Brassey Square, SW11. The doodlebug was heard to go over, but for some reason it circled back and hit houses across the road, falling in the rear garden of 2 Brassey Square. Fortunately, the family had moved to their Morrison shelter, because the whole front of the house was now lying in the street. Five residents were killed; over 100 houses were damaged or destroyed. The incident reports give an indication of how rescue efforts were organised after a raid. Five ambulances were despatched by 06.35, along with the warning that Bolingbroke Hospital was already full, followed by a further seven. Various mobile units were warned to expect up to 200 people; heavy casualties were feared. They were told to approach via Grayshott Road as all other routes were blocked by debris, with neighbouring areas being contacted for ambulance reinforcements. Eleven rescue parties were also sent, along with a mobile command unit. By 08.18, less than two hours after the impact, everything became calmer. The summary said: two killed, three still trapped, 32 taken to hospital [hence the need for ambulances] and 10 minor casualties. Final figures were: four dead (another casualty had been found later in the afternoon), 44 to hospital, 30-40 treated at a First Aid Post. The incident was closed at 12.28, six hours later. Just one incident among many, but this demonstrates the range of resources required and the amount of time taken to resolve an incident.

Dr R. V. Jones, ADI (Science), was living in a flat in Richmond and commuting to his office at 54 Broadway near St James's Park. Both areas were not without risk; Richmond had often been bombed during the earlier years of the war, while Broadway was near a number of key targets such as Whitehall and Westminster. On 17 July, a month after the main V1 raids began, he was concerned in case his intelligence knowledge might die with him.

"I wrote a note in case a flying bomb got me during the night instructing the finder:

> "[17 July 1944]. In case I am killed during the night of 17/18 July, whoever finds this paper must take it at once to Dr F C Frank, Government Communications Bureau, 54 Broadway, SW1 and tell him... [some key information about a V2 site at Blizna] .... [signed] RV Jones, ADI (Science), Air Ministry."

There were V1s again morning and evening on 18 July. Croydon suffered a number of attacks, with 142 V1s in three months and over 2,000 victims dead or injured. On this occasion, ten people were killed when a newsagent's shop on Brighton Road was hit; they were calling in for their morning papers or walking to work when the V1 struck.

At about 20.37 that evening, Tuesday 18 July 1944, a V1 flying bomb flew straight through the open doors of Elmers End Bus Garage in Beckenham and exploded near the entrance, blowing the roof off. An eyewitness described:

> "That sound was to haunt us for the rest of our lives, we suffered the trauma of hearing the approaching sound ... followed by those dreadful seconds of silence until the ear-shattering explosion came."

One of the engineering staff, John Cunningham, managed to sound the alarm bell to warn of the approaching flying bomb before he was killed. At least 17 civilians, possibly as many as 18, including ten members of London Transport staff, were killed. More than 40 others were injured, and 39 vehicles were damaged or destroyed. The dead included two members of the Home Guard Rescue Service, as well as an elderly woman in the street outside. The explosion caused several bus fuel tanks to explode, which ignited a large fire; a number of firemen were badly injured. 60 houses were damaged, with another 50 slightly damaged. Nevertheless, London Transport ran a full service the next day.

On the evening of 18 July, the Heinkel aircraft of III/KG3 flew 14 sorties from Rosières to launch V1s against London. All the Heinkels came back safely. V1s fell on Deptford Dockyard, Beckenham (which suggests the Elmers End Bus Garage V1 was air-launched) and Kennington. Yet more flying bombs came over that night, crossing Essex on their way to London. Over 45 V1s were shot down by RAF fighters over Kent and Sussex, while more were shot down into the sea by coastal anti-aircraft batteries. However, some V1s got through the defences, notably in Wandsworth and Peckham and as far west as Southall. These areas were bombed again the following day, 19 July, and 23 people were killed in three incidents.

The next night, 19/20 July, III/KG3 at Rosières flew 26 air-launched sorties, the first leaving at 22.46 and the last returning at 06.10, with no losses. Ten V1s reached north London at Edmonton and Enfield while others reached as far as Ealing, Feltham and Hammersmith.

By mid-July about 100 V1s a day were being launched, of which 25-30 were reaching the capital, and many of the rest were falling on the towns and villages between London and the coast. The Government had a dilemma; should they be economical with the truth, which was that the V1s were tending to fall short? Indeed, should they suggest to their agents that the range needed to be adjusted and in doing so engineer a further shortfall? In other words, suggest that the V1s (which tended to hit to the south of the Thames) were overshooting to the north. That way, by subterfuge, the V1s could be made to have a main point of impact in, for example, Dulwich, rather than Tower Bridge. There was a real dilemma about what to say: the truth or an engineered shortfall? This was hotly debated during July, but it was generally not felt to be a good thing, and any subterfuge was rejected. The Home Secretary asked, "Who are we to act as God?" Dr. Jones and his colleagues passionately attacked the deception policy. The general decision was to stay as things were.

Two German Messerschmitt fighters landed at RAF Manston on the night of 20/21 July at about 02.40, to the surprise of all concerned; they had mistaken it for a French airfield. Both pilots were taken prisoner.

At 06.54 on Friday 21 July a V1 hit Penge High Street, killing seven and damaging over 150 properties. (By the time the V1 campaign ended, it was said that every single building in Penge had suffered some damage, however slight.) Later Barchester Street in Bow was hit, killing a further seven. Deptford was hit twice in four hours, and there were several other V1s in east and southeast London, along with several in the Maidstone area.

There was another incident where a Metropolitan Police horse was later awarded the Dickin Medal, one of only two in this V1 campaign. Upstart was a chestnut gelding with four white feet and a blaze on his face. He had been stabled near Hyde Park until an attack on a nearby anti-aircraft station damaged his stable. He was then moved to East London and was patrolling a street in Bethnal Green with his rider DI J. Morley in July, a few weeks after the bombing at Tooting where Olga showed her bravery, when a bomb landed 75 feet in front of them, showering horse and rider with bits of glass and shrapnel. Upstart remained remarkably unconcerned and helped his rider in directing traffic and dealing with crowd control after the incident. He was awarded the Dickin Medal for courage during active duty.

On Saturday 22 July the Government announced that the number of flying bombs up to 06.00 that day was now 4,056. (This was up from 3,526 on 14 July, so just over another 500 in a week.) There had been a break of 5 nights (10/11–14/15 July) but after that London was the main target both night and day. 63 V1s hit London that day, including one that killed or injured 175 people in "the west of the capital".

Further air-launched flying bombs arrived in the early morning of 24 July. One hit Canterbury Terrace, Kilburn at 04.40 and killed 16 residents. Another four hit London. The remaining six doodlebugs blew up in Essex and Hertfordshire.

Later that day a V1 fell on Argyle Road, Teddington. The street had already been attacked on the night of 29 November 1940, the big raid on Teddington and Twickenham where over 60 people were killed. This time over 1,000 houses were damaged to some degree. There were 83 casualties including nine killed, and 15 seriously injured. Nearly the whole of Argyle Road was reduced to rubble.

During the night of 24/25 July, III/KG3 carried out 25 air-launched sorties from Gilze-Rijen between 22.05 and 05.24; all the aircraft returned safely. Six V1s hit London, three hit Hertfordshire and one Essex, but only light casualties were reported. Nevertheless, the air-launched V1s were now regularly hitting London from this date, albeit in smaller quantities than the former conventional V1 attacks.

In the early hours of 26 July, there were 18 alleged air launches from Gilze-Rijen, but possibly only eleven of these launched successfully. London, Essex and Hertfordshire each received three V1s, with some damage to property and some injuries.

Meanwhile, in a speech to Luftwaffe officers, Himmler boasted that the V1 attacks were very successful:

"Regarding the V1 fire, which is being kept up day and night without interruption – it is never known when it will come. A warning for southern England

and London is never possible, which is very nerve-wracking and costs a great number of lives. News from London indicates that London had 120,000 dead [sic] after four weeks.... Eleven million people are affected by this bombardment....This means that 25 per cent of the total English population is affected by this....It is something which in a military sense is weakening the power of a nation of a belligerent state."

The nightly air launches continued. A speculative report from British intelligence noted: "THE FLYING BOMBS ARE ACTUALLY LAUNCHED FROM THE AIRCRAFT!" [Their caps in report.] Clearly a surprise.

On the night of 26/27 July, III/KG3 flew another 19 sorties, this time from Roye-Amy in France; the unit there was equipped with He111s capable of air launching flying bombs against England. These caused casualties in Streatham, Clapham, Beckenham and Barking. There was one death at Great Warley, Essex; this was possibly the first V1 fatality in East Anglia.

On 27 July, there were more flying bombs around London. Twenty-four people were killed when a V1 fell in Church Road, Beckenham, with other V1s at West Norwood and Tulse Hill. A number of V1s were shot down near Maidstone; seven came down between 15.25 and 23.50. Another hit Eastbourne at 19.25, injuring 34. It is easy to assume that the deaths and injuries were as a result of direct hits, but many doodlebugs were shot down by fighters while en route to London. The interception success rate seems impressive; however, the V1s had to come to earth somewhere, and if they fell short of their target, they might still cause deaths and injuries. While generally the V1s would fall in a less populated area, the lack of an advance warning might result in more casualties. "One less for London" was the commonly held view, but one that was perhaps less easy to maintain if you were living in Doodlebug Alley.

A nearby V1: 27 July, Priory Road, Hounslow

There are so many doodlebug stories in World War Two, but this one is special to me; it is an incident in suburbia which happened very near my home. I moved here in the 1980s to one of the many 1930s semi-detached houses in Hounslow. A friend talked of her house survey, a few houses away from mine, where it mentioned "moderate damage; only one original ceiling (the front room, downstairs) and historic subsidence on back of kitchen due to nearby bombing in WW2." We were puzzled but thought no more about it.

A few years later, a colleague, Mark, visited me with his wife, Diana. They had walked up to my place via the alleyway at the end of the road; Diana said she was sure she recognised the area. There was a World War Two story attached to it. Eventually she began to recall more details, and this is what she told me.

Her paternal grandparents, Dorothy and Edward Elliott, used to live at number 79 Lyncroft Gardens, next to the last house. One day a doodlebug exploded barely 100 yards away. The force of the blast propelled the bath downstairs; luckily it was unoccupied at the time. Their pet lost the tip of its tail in the incident. This was the story she remembered being told as a child, maybe twenty years after the event, but she had no more details. I wanted to find out more.

The incident happened on Thursday 27 July. It was late afternoon in the school holidays, nearly five o'clock, when people heard a doodlebug coming closer, approaching from Heath Road to the north. It began to travel along the length of Lyncroft Gardens; it flew over number 6, then looked as though it was about to run out of fuel and crash. It hovered there, then juddered off southwards towards Priory Road.

The doodlebug crashed in the back garden of number 11 Priory Road. It exploded at 16.56, just before teatime. Many people were still at work and avoided the attack. However, from the pattern of the casualties, it looks as though the women and children were probably in the kitchens at the back of the houses and so closest to the blast.

Two little girls died at number 11: Lily Elizabeth Jackson aged 22 months and her sister Margaret Rose aged four. Number 13, the other half of the semi-detached house, also lost two children: David Goodgame aged 22 months and his brother John aged eight. John went to Chatsworth School, a couple of streets away. The next-door neighbour at number 9 Priory Road, Alice Amelia Hill, aged 66, also died.

Other neighbours were initially buried in the wreckage of their homes. One died later that day; Rosina Jefferson aged 48 of 136 Park Road was injured and died the same day in Hounslow Hospital, Heston. Park Road runs parallel to Priory Road, and the garden of number 136 backs on to that of number 11, where the doodlebug exploded; it would have suffered a considerable blast.

The total toll of dead and injured was: five died at the time, including four young children, and another died in hospital that day; 56 people were injured (16 seriously, 40 slightly). Nine houses were totally demolished; afterwards they were rebuilt in the original 1930s style. 69 houses were seriously damaged and a further 700 damaged. (I was told that the ceiling came down at number 6 Lyncroft Gardens with the force of the blast, and this was probably true for a number of other houses nearby, as my friend's survey suggests.) 70 people were rendered homeless.

All of this came from just one V1 that fell on a Thursday teatime in suburbia in the school holidays. Allegedly, "all casualties cleared within an hour … apart from some of those buried under debris"; there was a Heavy Mobile Unit in action at the corner of Lyncroft Gardens and Priory Road to help retrieve those trapped in the wreckage. The incident is also mentioned in the accident reports for Richmond and Twickenham as the roads involved are very close to the boundary; there are references to damage there, so it was clearly a significant event. Professor Lindemann's later suggestion that one doodlebug equated, on average, to one death is a clear underestimate, both in terms of damage sustained and the emotional impact on all those involved. There are no records of individual injuries, but even if you simply consider the effect on the lives of the 70 made homeless, it must have been devastating. These were close-knit neighbourhoods.

Later that night, III/KG3 flew 25 sorties from Rosières between 22.50 and 05.40; some crews flew twice. Three Heinkels were lost.

On Friday 28 July there was one of the worst single flying bomb incidents in south London. It happened at about 09.41 with no warning when a V1 hit the crowded town centre in Lewisham. It landed on the roof of a street level shelter outside a Marks & Spencer department store, causing major damage to the store and the Woolworths next to it as it exploded in the market area. Many were killed in the Woolworth's basement restaurant and two passing buses were ripped apart. Fifty-nine people died, then or later, and another 124 were very seriously injured. 178 were slightly injured, with a lot of damage from flying glass. The blast zone of this bomb stretched for 600 yards in all directions, damaging about 100 shops. Those who died were from a relatively narrow radius; most had lived within two or three miles of Lewisham town centre.

The day was made even worse when another 45 were killed in Kensington High Street in central London at 13.30, during the lunch hour. A further 170 were injured, 54 seriously and 116 slightly. The V1 hit the J. Lyons Café at the corner of Earls Court Road and Kensington High Street. It was the biggest single death toll in Kensington that summer.

In just under four hours those two incidents caused 104 deaths and injured 472 people. These were not the only deaths that day; the V1s continued to fall. Sometimes the air launches coincided with the land launching from Northern France. The results varied considerably, both in accuracy and in scope.

There were further incidents on 28 and 29 July. A V1 in Elephant & Castle partly destroyed two surface shelters and killed five people. Later on 29 July there was a cricket match at Lord's, where the Army were playing the RAF in front of over 3,000 spectators. Fortunately, the bomb fell short and play continued.

The night of 29/30 July saw many sorties from Rosières, possibly as many as 31, with some flown twice. On Sunday 30 July at 11.30, a V1 hit Taunton Road, Swanscombe village; it wiped out half of one side of the road. It killed 13, seriously injured 22, and injured another 69. Eight houses were demolished and 150 people made homeless.

The following night there were at least 20 sorties from III/KG3, in two waves. Nine Heinkels left at about 23.30, then another 11 at 02.55. Later analysis suggested most of the first batch were launched off Blankenberge; some of the later ones came from off Walcheren. Eight V1s hit London, two other V1s fell in Essex. One hit Greenwich, killing two and injuring 53.

On 31 July Thornton Heath had another V1, killing 1 and wrecking many houses.

On the night of 31 July/1 August, 23 sorties took off from Gilze-Rijen between 22.16 and 04.15. Some of these V1s may have been launched off Ostend, while others may have been from the Dutch islands.

There had been more than 350 sorties flown since operations had begun on the night of 3/4 July. Eight Heinkels had been lost during the month, with two more damaged on the ground. What would August bring?

Chapter 4

August 1944: The Height of the Assault

August brought the first real sun of the summer, but the raids continued; soon it became cold and wet again. By August 50% of V1s were destroyed before they could reach London, thanks to a combination of anti-aircraft guns and night fighters. Nevertheless, during the first week alone 395 people were killed in London and 57 elsewhere. During the second week there were no fewer than 459 flying bombs; the third week was more challenging still with 700, and in the final week, while the number dropped, it was still 550. Many accounts state that August was "the height of the assault". The Prime Minister, Winston Churchill, remarked "The Angel of Death is abroad in the land, only you can't always hear the flutter of its wings."

While some of the V1s would have been traditionally launched, an increasing number were air-launched from Heinkel 111 aircraft; the radar tracks confirmed this, as many bombs were launched from an East-West axis.

On the night of 1/2 August there were 12 air-launched sorties from Gilze-Rijen between 21.54 and 00.25, with no losses.

The next day the Prime Minister gave a progress report, saying 5,735 V1s had been launched "upon us" with a "wholesale destruction of homes". The damage to property was another aspect of the V1 campaign; one flying bomb could easily damage over a hundred homes.

At 13.02 on 2 August, a V1 hit a restaurant, Richard's Café on Beckenham Road, near the railway line. It was crowded with people having lunch. 44 people were killed, many instantly, with twenty more badly injured. There was a lot of damage from glass, and the blast ripped the top deck off a passing bus and tore apart another one; some of the passengers emerged with their clothing set alight. The Prince Arthur pub nearby was demolished. Shops and houses lining the road suffered huge destruction; there was severe damage to 60 shops and houses, with 140 more slightly damaged. This was one of the worst V1 incidents in South London; for the borough of Beckenham, it was the worst civilian incident of the war. Allegedly by this stage of the V1 attacks the Nazis were packing the flying bombs with more powerful explosives, though this is hard to prove; the V1 which hit the Co-op Stores in Camberwell on 5 August was also felt to be significantly more destructive than others.

Herbert Steer, aged 56, was just one of those who died at the restaurant. Little more than two weeks before, his 17-year-old son Sydney had died when another V1 hit Elmers End bus garage on 18 July. Just two among so many V1 deaths, but it makes you realise how families could be affected by a range of V1 attacks as they went about their day-to-day lives.

There was a single air-launched raid with about 15 V1s at about 02.45 that night. About five V1s reached the London area and two fell as far west as Brentford and Staines; the air launches were clearly able to reach West London.

On Thursday 3 August, a barrack block and five accommodation huts were demolished at RAF Hendon when they were hit by a V1 in the early hours; five airmen were killed and over 25 wounded. It is worth remembering that the military were also at risk while serving in the UK. Incidents such as Sloane Court, Newlands and the Guards' Chapel all demonstrated this; civilians were not the only targets for V1s.

During the morning, the area round Maidstone received a number of V1s. One fell near Maidstone West station after snagging the wires of a barrage balloon. It killed five workmen on the railway, severely injured a further ten people, most of whom had to be hospitalised, and slightly injured 40, with considerable damage to houses and shops.

Later that day, at about 12.30, a young French pilot, Captain Jean Maridor (1920-1944) of the RAF 91st Squadron took off on what was to be his last mission; he was passionate about flying and had obtained his private pilot's licence at the age of 17, before coming to England in 1940 to join the RAF. He had received the Croix de Guerre and DFC (Distinguished Flying Cross) and by summer 1944 he began to specialise in chasing V1s.

He spotted a V1 near Rye and gave chase in his Spitfire. He made repeated attempts to shoot it down as it travelled north, then realised that it was likely to hit Benenden School, by then in use as a large war time hospital; this would cause great damage to both the hospital and the village. With less than 50 metres between him and the V1, which was by now closing in on the hospital, he let off a final salvo with his cannon. The doodlebug exploded; this tore off the right wing of his Spitfire, which then plummeted to the ground. He died in the crash; his remains were found close by the hospital, surrounded by the remains of the V1. His was a heroic death and he probably saved many lives. He had been due to marry his fiancée, WAAF Section Officer Jean Lambourn, on Friday 11 August; they were looking forward to living in France after the war.

At 11.05 on 3 or 4 August 1944 (accounts differ – the plaque in the church says 4 August, but several personal accounts suggest 3 August) a V1 flying bomb destroyed Tidebrook School near Wadhurst, Sussex. Fortunately, there were no serious casualties as the older children had made it to an Anderson shelter in time, while the younger ones had sheltered in the playground. Six people were injured. The school was badly damaged and was never rebuilt.

The accounts above are just a few of those incidents logged for that day, but they indicate the wide range of attacks that occurred.

On the night of 4/5 August, the Hythe anti-aircraft battery began to shoot down V1s, starting at 01.00. By the next morning no fewer than 17 had been shot down into the sea.

The following day, Bank Holiday Saturday, 5 August, a V1 landed on the Royal Arsenal Co-op Stores in Lordship Lane, Camberwell, at 16.45. The shop was crowded with weekend shoppers and there were long queues outside waiting for the trams home. When the V1 exploded, the tram queue was "cut to pieces". 23 people died and 43 were seriously injured. The rescue squads worked for two days and through the night to recover the victims. The damage extended across a 700-yard radius, greater than the normal blast area. It was one of the worst events in South London in 1944.

Later that day, at 18.58, a V1 was brought down by a Tempest aircraft and landed in Malling Road, Snodland; the explosion killed 12 people and demolished 10 houses in the village. A further 16 people were badly injured and 17 slightly injured; two doctors, whose surgery facility was within one of the houses, carried on treating the casualties, despite their own severe injuries. One was a Czech refugee who was cut by glass, while another doctor was hit by blast. The V1 might otherwise have continued on its course and hit Maidstone with far worse casualties if it had not been intercepted.

That night there were 22 air-launched sorties from Rosières, with several deaths when V1s fell in Southeast London.

A confidential report was issued that day, stating: "It is now known that flying bombs are being launched by He 111 aircraft operating from the Dutch/Belgian area. It is estimated that there are some 30-35 He 111s at present being used of which probably about 25 would be operational at any one time" .... "Activity from this area started on the morning of 8 July and has continued intermittently since then." ... "Scale of effort has been up to a maximum of 24 flying bombs spread over 7 hours of darkness, generally in two phases, and emanating from an area stretching from Ostend to Walcheren Island."

On Sunday 6 August anti-aircraft batteries were in action throughout the day, bringing down V1 flying bombs; the beaches along the coast at Folkestone and Hythe were becoming littered with wreckage from the doodlebugs. The fighter squadrons were busy too, with the Polish 316 squadron bringing down 9 V1s near Hastings. Later that day, at 17.10, a V1 flying bomb caused massive damage when it exploded in Carrington Road in East Hill, Dartford. Ten people died, 20 were admitted to hospital, with another 95 slightly injured. 20 homes were wrecked, and another 700 houses needed repair.

Tunbridge Wells, which lay beneath five or six regular V1 routes to London, somehow escaped the worst effects. Thousands of bombs passed over the town but only six fell on the Borough, causing two fatalities, one of which was a horse. The man who died was George Gearing of Stanley Road. That Sunday afternoon, 6th August, he was sitting in a small, thatched summerhouse on Tunbridge Wells Common, watching fighters overhead chasing two V1s. They were both shot down, one crashing at Pembury Road and the other on the Common near the Spa Hotel, close to George who was injured in the blast and died later in hospital.

The next night, 6/7 August, there were another 22 sorties from Rosières but with no losses; there were another 23 sorties the following night.

Increasing numbers of V1 flying bombs were being shot down. The fighter pilots were now trying hard to avoid shooting down V1s on built-up areas. There was an additional problem in that the bombs tended to fly erratically when hit, so that the fighter pilots could not predict where the V1s would eventually land.

On 9 August a V1 flying bomb exploded in the air above Lamberhurst; as it blew up, it scattered a number of 1-kilogram incendiary bombs, which was unusual. By now most V1s were coming over at night. For example, there were 25 sorties from Rosières on the night of 11/12 August, all between the hours of 22.04 and 02.13. 11 V1s were brought down by AA guns.

The American *Time* magazine described the VI campaign:

> "The 'Things' came over in increasing salvos. The number of robobombs destroyed in southern England's elaborate and still-growing system of defense rose; but more and more got through."

It talked about the three lines of defence for London, describing it as "triple-decked". When first identified, the approaching V1's course was plotted, and its trajectory planned. If it reached the English coast, it was attacked by ack-ack guns. If it got through these, it reached a wide belt of fighter planes. After that, the next defence would be a balloon barrage. Nevertheless, some V1s did get through by sheer force of numbers, despite the increasing success of the various elements of defence.

The chief problem for the fighters came from the fact that almost all activity was now carried out in darkness. It was easy to assume that intercepting V1s at night would be easier than in daylight simply because the tongue of flame emerging from the back of the bomb was so conspicuous in the dark. Unfortunately, merely seeing the bomb was not enough: pilots had also to estimate its range, and this proved extremely difficult. Sir Thomas Merton, the distinguished spectroscopist, designed a simple rangefinder which was very helpful to pilots; nevertheless, individual skill and experience remained the most critical factors.

On 12 August, No. 402 Squadron RCAF, flying Spitfire XIV fighters, began anti-V1 flying bomb operations in England. The squadron was based at RAF Hawkinge in Kent.

Later that night, there was an all-out effort from III/KG3 from Rosières; they made 36 sorties, possibly in two batches. A V1 landed on West Norwood at 01.30 and killed eight; another caused more deaths in Peckham, and there was some damage in rural Suffolk when a V1 hit a tree.

During the Sunday night of 13/14 August, Heinkel aircraft from III/KG3 launched 19 V1 flying bombs against Britain, a far smaller number than the previous evening. The Gruppe needed to leave their base at Rosières-en-Santerre, Picardy, because the Allied advance was approaching the area. The Heinkels were moving to Venlo in the Netherlands, but as a result could not launch any further bombs for a week. Nevertheless, more V1s (presumably air-launched) continued to arrive from other bases. A further seventeen V1 flying bombs were shot down by anti-aircraft fire.

On 14 August the US 127th Anti-Aircraft Artillery Regiment became operational; by the end of the next few weeks the regiment had accounted for 56 flying bombs. A V1 flying bomb brought down by anti-aircraft guns tragically fell on Twiss Road, Hythe in Kent, destroying houses and killing a family of five; it also injured a further 17, some seriously.

During the night of 14/15 August, the anti-aircraft guns were very busy around Folkestone and Hythe; 16 Divers were shot down into the sea.

There were a number of incidents on 15 August. At 16.45 in Rochester, a house was hit by a V1. Four people were killed, one seriously injured and 21 slightly injured. One house was demolished and there was superficial damage to no fewer than 600 others. This is just one example of the potential wide-ranging effects and damage from a single V1.

Later that evening a V1 fell on a large house in Shoot-up Hill near Kilburn Underground station. There were many casualties at the time, some later dying from their injuries. A fourteen-year-old boy (Ben Sachs) described: "The… most horrendous incident that I can remember was on the night of 15 August 1944 when a V1 flying bomb fell on some big houses in Shoot-Up-Hill… There were many casualties, and dead and injured people had to be dug out of the wreckage. I was given the job of being a runner to "Mick Rogers", the Head of Willesden's Civil Defence Rescue Service, who was in charge of directing rescue operations (he later received a George Medal for his work). Thirteen people died that night, and it was my first ever sight of dead bodies – something I shall never forget." Five members of the Brooks family and three of the Melachrino family (Carlos and Ulysse and their mother Hilda) died there. (George, Hilda's husband, was a well-known musician; he led the orchestra at the Café de Paris and became the conductor of the British Band of the Allied Expeditionary Forces.) The blast broke windows in buildings more than half a mile away.

On Wednesday 16 August a V1 flying bomb exploded in Hoe Street, Walthamstow, just before 10.00; it killed 22 people and seriously injured 62, causing a total of 144 casualties. It was a sunny August day, and many locals were out doing their shopping. They were swift to take cover, otherwise the total would have been higher. The blast wrecked a bus, killing the driver and injuring many passengers. It was not until after midnight that the full extent of the incident could be understood. Half of all the V1 casualties in Walthamstow were caused by this one incident.

During the day, Hythe reported that 30 V1s had been shot down into the sea, with another six just offshore; Folkestone gunners got a dozen.

Later that afternoon, after about 15.30, there was a shocking incident involving a V1 and a train. A doodlebug heading towards London was tipped by a fighter. It crashed to the ground and exploded near the railway bridge over Oak Lane, Newington. The blast destroyed the bridge, just before the packed 15.35 Victoria to Ramsgate express train was due; it left a large gap in the track. The train was unable to stop despite the efforts of the driver and fireman. The engine tender and the first three coaches hit the gap where the bridge had stood; the fourth coach hung across the track but didn't fall. The driver applied the emergency brake, while the fireman ran back to the Newington signal box to alert them to the incident. He was met there by a Home Guard officer. Seven passengers from the first three coaches were killed, along with a railway platelayer. Several passengers were thrown out of the carriages by the impact. Doctors, ambulances and the WVS were soon on the scene. Rainham School was used as a first aid post, with the transport café (the Rest Tea Rooms) nearby used as a hospital. Casualties were eventually taken to St Bartholomew's Hospital, Rochester, for emergency treatment. Fortunately, the driver and fireman were only slightly injured. It took two days to repair the bridge; then the line returned to normal.

The two trains would normally pass each other just about at the spot where the accident occurred. The up train was delayed, however, and was still standing at Newington station, about a mile down the line. It was the most serious accident in the area in WW2.

There seems to have been quite a lot of confusion in accounts about this incident. The date was given variously as 16 or 18 August; however, the victims' deaths are given as 16 August in *Ancestry (www.ancestry.co.uk)*. The train may have held 600 or 400 people, according to different accounts. The number of victims is given in one account as nine killed, 34 injured. Another version states eight killed, 33 seriously injured and taken to hospital and 28 slightly hurt. Yet another story states that about 100 were treated for minor injuries.

On 17 August at Folkestone, anti-aircraft gunners using proximity fused shells brought down 27 flying bombs during the day, all landing in the sea close to the beaches. The batteries at nearby Hythe accounted for a further 16, also mainly due to the proximity fuses. As usual the sheer number of bombs being launched meant that some got through to the London area and some places were hit several times over a period of days. There was a serious V1 incident at 15.30; 28 people from Mossbury Road in Lavender Hill were killed. Twelve died at the time, with 16 of the 25 seriously injured dying later. Many shops and dwellings were damaged.

V1s continued to arrive over the next few days. On 19 August a V1 flying bomb went astray and crashed near RAF Thorpe Abbots, the base of the 100th Bomber Group, with little warning. The base

Diagram of How to Construct an Anderson Shelter. (National Archives – OGL (Open Government License))

FIGURE 3

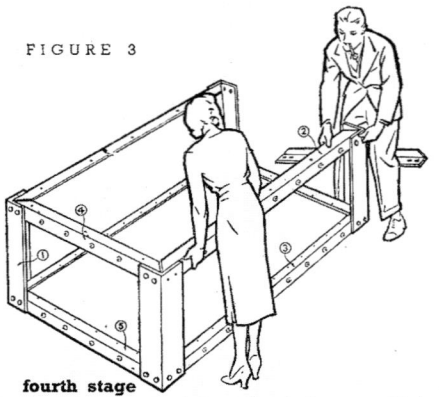

fourth stage

Put the top plate on the shelter. Use the lever provided so as to make the holes in the top plate fit exactly over the holes in the rails; as each one fits into place bolt it loosely with the 16 smaller bolts, with bolt head on top.

FIGURE 4

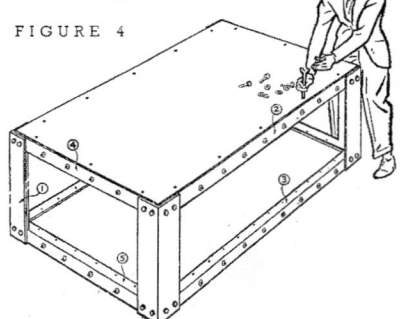

seventh stage

Put the side and end panels over the studs.

Get inside just before the last one is put into place, and fix the four hook-and-eye fastenings as shown in Figure 7. You

FIGURE 6

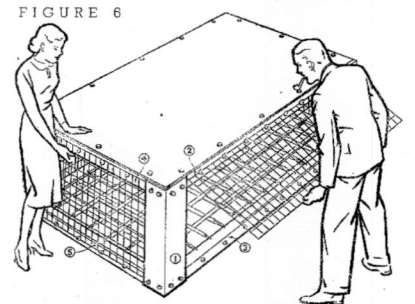

will notice in the illustration that the eyepiece is fastened to the last wire of the end covering; the hook-piece, however, is

How to Use the Shelter as a Table

FIGURE 8

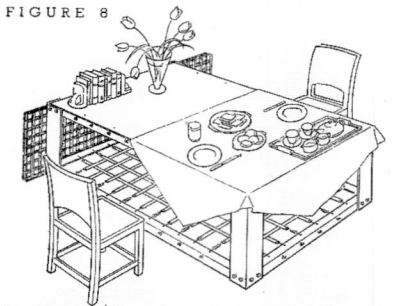

The side and end panels must be in place and fastened with the hook and eye fastenings, when the shelter is in use as such. To use it as a table, or to make the bed, the panels can be removed.

(25096.) 59985. Wt. 8557-P1089. 250,400. 4/41. A., P. & S., Ltd.

Extract from "How To Put Up Your Morrison Shelter". (National Archives OGL License (Open Government))

FLYING BOMB

FZG 76

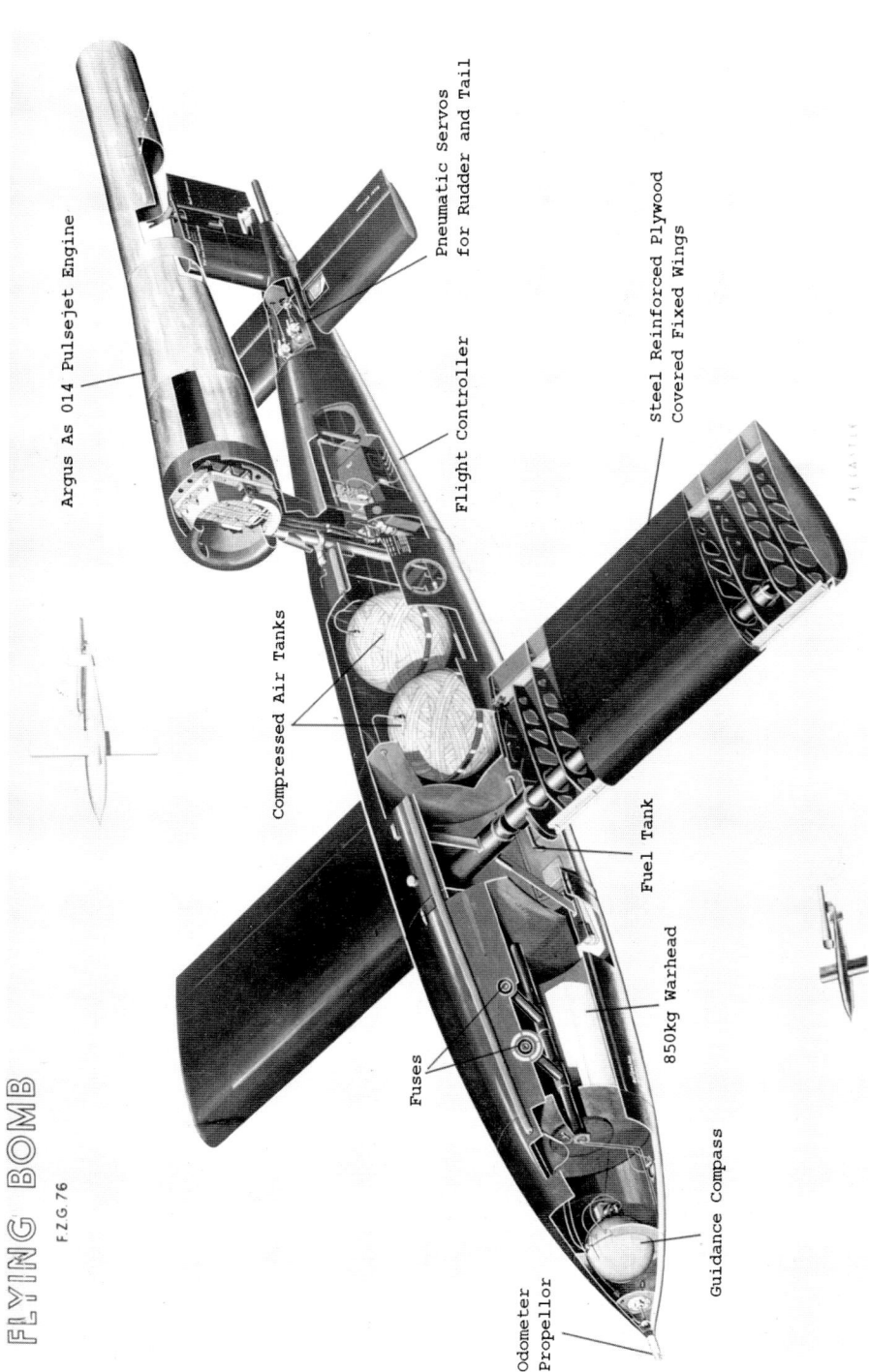

Argus As 014 Pulsejet Engine

Pneumatic Servos
for Rudder and Tail

Flight Controller

Steel Reinforced Plywood
Covered Fixed Wings

Compressed Air Tanks

Fuel Tank

850kg Warhead

Fuses

Guidance Compass

Odometer
Propellor

V1 Cutaway, annotated, US Air Force. (Public Domain)

V1 on Reconstructed Launch Ramp at IWM, Duxford. (CC BY SA 4.0 License, Photo by geni)

Heinkel HE 111 with V1 mounted under wing; video footage of an air launch can be seen at CriticalPast (www.criticalpast.com) (Public Domain).

Above: V1 being rolled to the launch site. (CC BY SA 3.0 de Bundesarchiv)

Right: Blue Plaque on Grove Road London marking the site of the first V1 to hit London on 13th June 1944. (CC-ASA 4.0 License Photo by Spudgun67)

ENGLISH HERITAGE

THE FIRST
FLYING BOMB
ON LONDON
FELL HERE.
13 JUNE 1944

F EMERGENCY

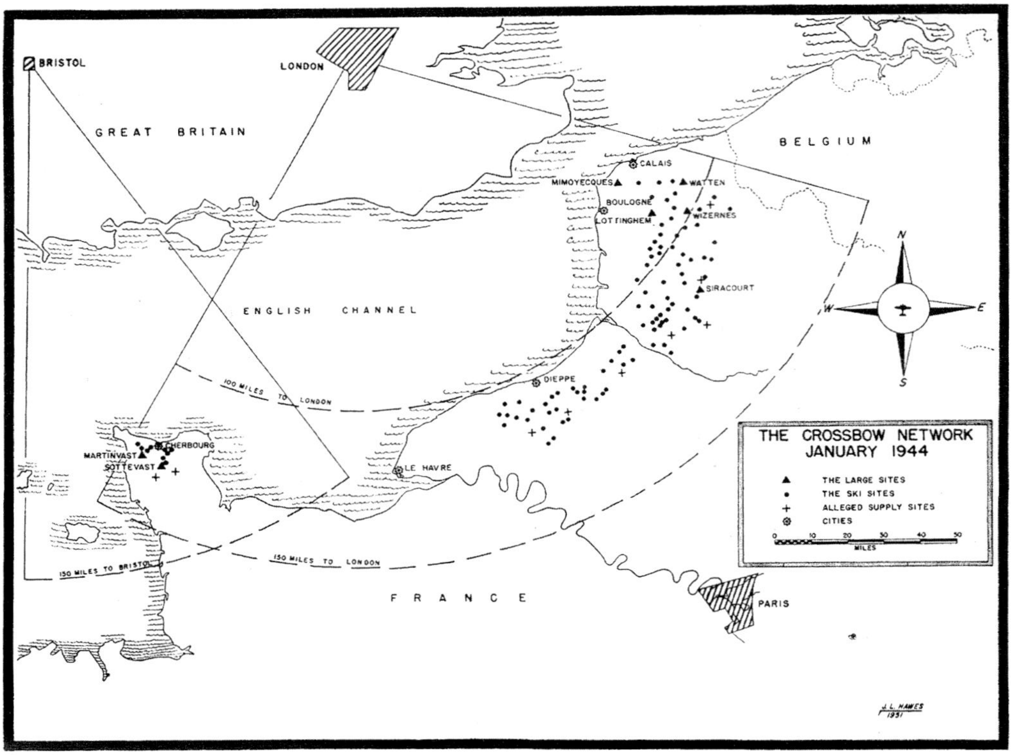

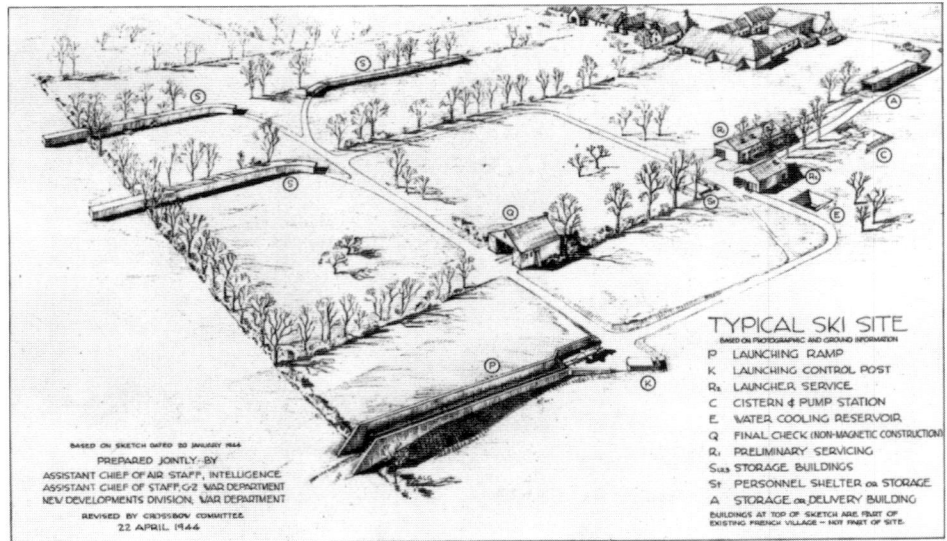

Map of Areas targeted in 'Operation Crossbow' bombing raids on sites believed to be being set up by the Germans to launch secret 'V' weapons. "Ski sites" refer to ramp launchers as pictured in reconstruction at IWM Duxford, US Air Force. (Public Domain)

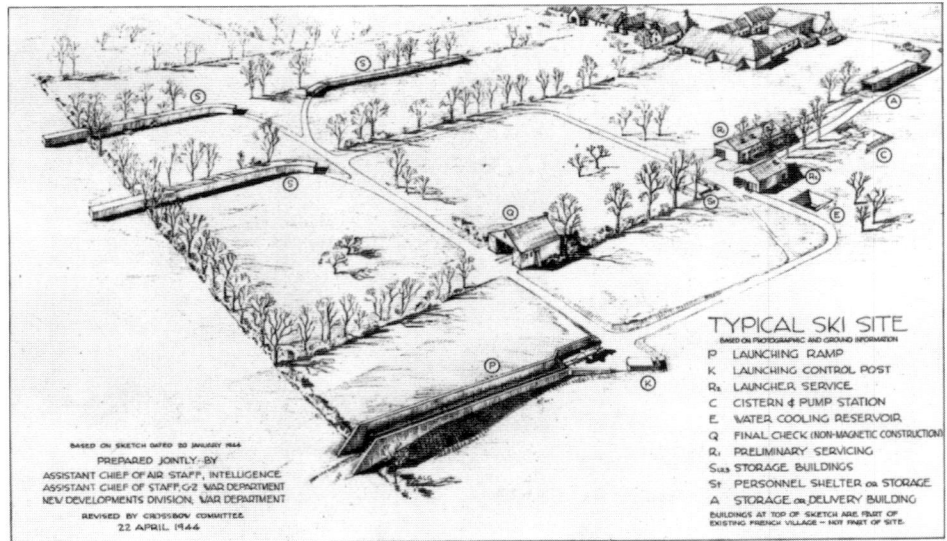

"Typical Ski Site" sketch depicting how a launch site might look, part of planning for 'Operation Crossbow', US Air Force. (Public Domain)

V1 Impact Crater at Crooked Yard Farm, Macclesfield Forest. This would have been an air launched V1 probably targeting Manchester that went off course. It caused injuries and some property damage but no fatalities. (Copyright Colin Park, Creative Commons CC-BYSA-2.0 License)

Drumhead Service outside the Guards' Chapel on 25th June 1944, a week after the bombing. (Crown Copyright)

Devastation within the chapel. (David Gurney)

Remains of the Guards' Chapel. (Crown Copyright)

Grave of Joan Duncan and Edith Farmer, both of HMS Copra, who died at the Guards' Chapel and were buried in the same grave in Romford. (Association of Wrens)

Above left: Bertha Massey Gleghorn, Britain's first Woman Police Officer to die in the line of duty after a V1 struck the police station in Tottenham Court Road on 19 June 1944. (Copyright UK Police Memorial)

Above right: Portrait of 401713 Flying Officer Dick Smith, of Brighton, Victoria, a member of No. 196 Squadron, died at the Aldwych, Australian War Memorial. (Public Domain)

Left: Portrait of Ground staff (Fitter) (Flight Sergeant Oswald 'Ossie' Ferguson, BEM) who also died at the Aldwych, Australian War Memorial. (Public Domain)

Below: Imber Court Welsh Guards Commemoration Details. (Copyright Imber Court)

Welsh 🏵 Guards

Training Battalion Commemoration Imber Court
30th June 1944

During the Second World War, the Training Battalion Welsh Guards were stationed in Sandown Park. On the 30th June 1944 the battalion held its annual athletics event at Imber Court. During the course of the day a German V1 Flying Bomb landed on the centre of the race track, the explosion causing many deaths and serious injuries.

In 1994 a small garden of remembrance was founded in memory of those who were killed. In 2001 the regiment inaugurated a memorial stone made of Welsh slate, upon which are recorded the names of the eighteen Welsh Guardsmen and two other service personnel killed.

A remembrance service is commemorated at Imber Court on the last Sunday in June each year.

Welsh Guards

2nd Lt. G A M Baker
3769857 Gdsm. C W Bristow
2nd Lt. J A L Crofts
2739165 Gdsm. A Fernihough
2739388 Gdsm. J F Fernyhough
6145541 Gdsm. C C Field
2739223 Gdsm. I G Glen
3778234 Gdsm. G H Green
2734026 Sgt. T G Griffiths
2737388 Gdsm. A G Hill
14372843 Gdsm. J T Hughes
2738924 Gdsm. S E Jones

Welsh Guards

2731946 CSM C H Lang
14295068 Gdsm. A E Lemon
Lt. W F Moss
6468155 LCpl. C Richardson
2739424 Gdsm. A F Street
2739402 Gdsm. H Wheeler

Army Physical Training Corps

2656228 CSM I W Thompson

ATS

W/148928 Pte. J E Jefferies

Private Margaret Hicks of the ATS, a member of a mixed anti-aircraft battery on the South Coast, paints another V1 'kill' on the battery scoreboard, 6th August 1944. (Lt O'Brien, Public Domain)

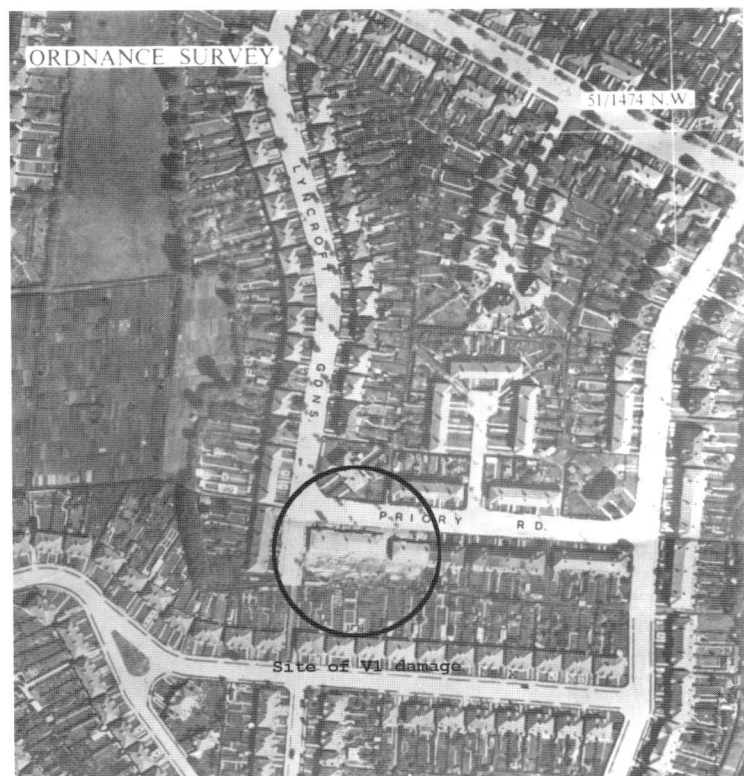

Site of V1 damage on Priory Road, Hounslow, visible in Ordnance Survey Aerial Photograph taken in 1947. (CC-BY National Library of Scotland)

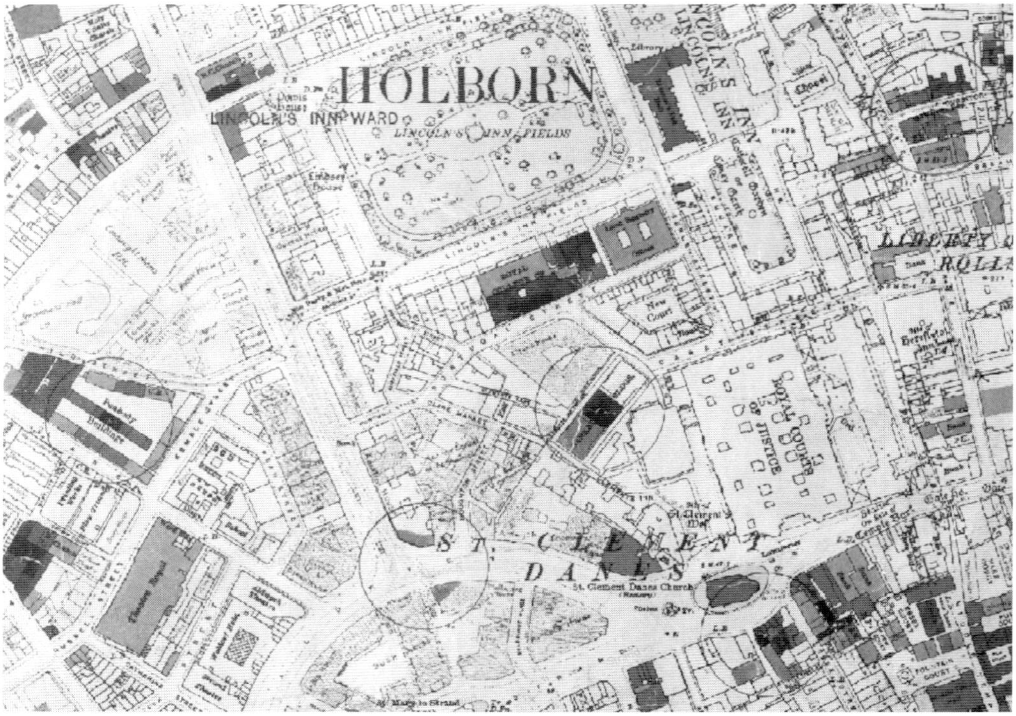

Above: London County Council Bomb Damage Map Showing Area around Aldwych (St Clement Danes) in which 5 Vls (denoted by circles) fell during the war. The circle in the centre shows the site of the Aldwych bomb of 30 June. Purple shading denotes damage beyond repair whilst black shading shows total destruction. (London Metropolitan Archives)

Left: Jean Maridor, French Pilot who died shooting down a Vl, 3rd August 1944. (Public Domain)

Right: Constance Babington Smith analyses reconnaissance photos with a stereoscopic viewer; she was one of the first to spot the V1 launch sites. (Crown Copyright)

Below: Casualty No. 1, a painting by Louis Duffy (1940), depicting the rescue services following a raid. (Out of Copyright)

Above: Olga and Upstart who won the Dickin medal for bravery in 1947 for their conduct when dealing with V1s in 1944. Photo is of from left to right: Olga, Regal and Upstart with their handlers at the Dickin Medal ceremony in 1947. (Dickin Medal Archives)

Left: Destruction of the Rex Cinema in Antwerp, where 567 people were killed when a V2 rocket exploded. (NARA National Archives and Records Administration)

A photograph of a V1 flying overhead taken near Antwerp. (© Jan B.H.A. Vervloedt. (CC-BY-SA 3.0)

A captured V1 on display towards the end of the war in Antwerp. (CC-BY-SA 4.0 Tlford2035)

Barrage balloons over Buckingham Palace, London, during the war. (Crown Copyright)

A restored anti-aircraft gun at Mudchute Park, Isle of Dogs. (CC-BY-SA 3.0 By Leutha)

diarist commented that, "The tannoy gave a red alert and two seconds later the buzz bomb blew."

Further V1s continued to be shot down during the night of 19/20 August; the AA gunners at Hythe shot down 12 V1s while Folkestone colleagues got another 18 in the 12 hours up to 06.00.

On 20 August a V1 landed on an air raid shelter in The Close, Hanworth at lunchtime, killing 11 and injuring 13, many of whom were just leaving. Although the V1 attacks had reduced in intensity, they continued to cause significant casualties.

On Monday 21 August at 12.47 Willesden in north-west London received its second V1 flying bomb in two days; this hit College Road, where 20 were killed and 29 injured. That evening at 20.17, 29 people died and 58 were sent to hospital in Wharncliffe Gardens, Marylebone. Meanwhile the anti-aircraft battery in Dover had their most successful day yet, shooting down more than 36 bombs over the sea and beaches.

My family and the Churchfield Road V1

My mother would never tell me the story of her friends and the Guards' Chapel V1 (see chapter 2 for more details). However, she was less reluctant to tell me about the bomb that narrowly missed my grandparents' house in Acton. My paternal grandparents, William and Bertha Mitchell, were running a shoe repair business in Acton early in the war; their previous enterprise had been in Bute Street, Kensington. The new shop was at 108 Churchfield Road; I can remember the layout from my visits as a small child in the 1950s. The shop was downstairs, fronting onto the pavement, with the dining room behind it and the scullery and kitchen behind that. It looked across the road to a graveyard, complete with gravestones, something that gave me the horrors as an over-imaginative small child; you had an even better view of the Churchfield Road Burial Ground from the upstairs sitting room window.

It was Monday lunchtime on 21 August. My father Alan was staying with his parents for a few days; he would normally have been in Christchurch on the South Coast, where he had been working for the scientific civil service for just over a year. My mother Enid had just graduated from Kings and was about to start a teaching post at Bristol in a few weeks' time, away from the dangers of London. I imagine she was still staying at the YWCA in Penywern Road, Earls Court, just as she had been at the time of the Guards' Chapel incident in June, when she had lost three friends to a V1. She was visiting my father and his parents; she and Dad had met in their first term at University in November 1942 and by now had an "understanding".

My grandfather would have been serving in the shop; my grandmother was at the back of the house, preparing lunch. My mother and father were upstairs in the sitting room, ready to come down for a meal; they were chatting when they suddenly heard the distinctive sound of an approaching doodlebug. Mum immediately recognised it and froze; at that point the engine noise stopped. Dad was quick to take action. He leapt up, grabbed Mum, and pulled them both behind the settee to take shelter from the threat of broken glass. A scant few seconds later, at 13.15, there was a loud explosion followed by clouds of smoke; the windows were blown in. Downstairs Grandpa had ducked below the shop counter to avoid the slivers of glass; Grandma was in the scullery and had dived into the Morrison shelter there.

Once they had checked that Grandma and my mother were uninjured, albeit shaken, Grandpa and my Dad set off towards the park to check what had happened. The V1 had exploded at the far end of Churchfield Road, just beyond Acton Central Station at the entrance to Acton Park. There was heavy damage and a lot of smoke, and Heavy Rescue vehicles were starting to arrive. The four houses, numbers 4-10 Churchfield Road East between the station and the entrance to the park, had been severely damaged. Five people were killed, three at number 8 and one at number 6, with an air raid warden killed by blast in the street outside. Two people were deemed missing, with seven seriously injured and 16 slightly injured. This was the last of the seven V1s that fell on Acton.

My grandparents would presumably have known several of the killed and wounded as they had been living and working in Churchfield Road for several years. Number 4 Churchfield Road East was the home of the Nelhams family; they had to move elsewhere in Acton after the raid as the house was destroyed, but Grandma often spoke to me about Terry Nelhams, better known as Adam Faith, the popstar, who was born at number 4. There is a plaque to him at the entrance to the park.

On the night of 21/22 August, III/KG3 of the German Air Force launched 21 sorties with air-launched V1s between 21.50 and 02.00 from their new base at Venlo in the southeast of the Netherlands; they had taken a week's break after their move from Rosières. There were few casualties, but areas hit included Brentwood, West Ham, Willesden, Pirbright and Hartlip, near Rainham. All the Heinkel bombers returned safely after launching their flying bombs, apart from one which crashed on take-off. One of these bombs hit half a mile down Oak Lane, where the railway bridge had just been repaired after the explosion on 16 August with the train.

The following night the AA defences did well; Folkestone shot down eight V1s and Hythe hit 18, all of which fell into the sea.

In France, the battle for the liberation of Paris lasted from 19 to 25 August. There were victory peals in London on 24 August at St Paul's and Westminster Abbey at 16.00, which were slightly premature. The garrison did not surrender until 25 August, when General de Gaulle assumed control of the city.

By the end of the month British and Canadian troops were advancing towards the Pas de Calais, which made the units of F155(W) withdraw eastwards towards previously prepared ski sites in Holland; by late August there was only one battery left in action in Pas de Calais. In theory, until these sites were fully operational, London was supposed to be out of range of the relocated V1s. By now the anti-aircraft guns had destroyed more than 1,500 flying bombs.

But the V1 attacks continued. The last major incident involving a factory took place on 23 August at Standard Telephones and Cables Ltd at New Southgate. It was a large factory complex consisting of several three-storey buildings. The factory made a wide range of items for the war effort: Bailey bridges, teleprinters, tank and fighter radios, transceivers and many others. Because these were essential to the war, the STC employees would normally carry on working until the last possible moment when there was an alert. The workers relied on lookouts on the roof. A yellow alert was announced over the tannoy if there was a raid; they would just carry on working. If there was a red alert, this meant danger was quite close and the workers would normally lie down on the floor next to the machines as there was no time to reach the air raid shelters.

It was a dull misty morning; visibility was poor with low cloud. The lookouts were keeping an eye on a V1 as it came closer, and the red alert had already sounded. Suddenly they saw it just short of the main gate. One spotter yelled desperately "Lie down! For God's sake, lie down!" At 07.59, the flying bomb exploded on Building 7 in the heart of the factory. It blew a crater four feet deep and twelve feet wide and Buildings 6 and 8 took the full force of the blast.

A woman operating the multi-spindle drilling machines on the ground floor of the building nearest the gates said that the explosion could be heard clearly, despite the sound of the machinery. The next thing the women heard was a shaky voice which said, "Switch off the machines, take your handbags and go down to the shelters." These air raid shelters were on the other side of the roadway from their building. All the volunteer firemen and rescue people were then asked to report for duty. The woman and her colleagues made their way out, guessing the incident had been quite close; to their horror, they saw that the camouflage netting (which covered the Radio building) was burning fiercely, and many windows were broken. The "wood shop" had ceased to exist; it had taken the brunt of the blast. A V1 had fallen between the Radio building and the Wood shop.

No further workers were allowed to enter the area. The works fire brigade was quick to start controlling the numerous fires, while the in-house medical team began to deal with the injured. The rescue workers began to extricate those who were trapped. All other workers were encouraged to go home at lunchtime; many went to pass messages to their family and friends in an attempt to reassure them.

The final death toll was 33, of whom 21 died on the spot; about 210 were seriously injured. It was one of the highest of the whole campaign; the Aldwych death toll was about 50, with at least 200 seriously injured, while the Guards' Chapel total was 124 dead, with 141 seriously injured.

That night, 23/24 August, the guns at Folkestone brought down 14 V1s, while Hythe AA got another 20.

On 24 August at 19.52 a heavy anti-aircraft gun position in Anerley Road, Penge took a direct hit from a V1 flying bomb; it killed all seven of the gun crew, believed to have been Home Guard soldiers. However, the anti-aircraft guns along the coast at Folkestone and Hythe had another successful day, thanks to their proximity fused shells which shot down over 65 flying bombs into the sea before they reached the mainland. Small boys on their bicycles began to enjoy seeing the bombs get hit and explode on a regular basis; they would then cycle to the impact sites along the coast in the hope of collecting parts of the bombs as trophies before the Home Guard arrived to stop them. A spark plug was the most coveted find.

By 25 August the number of V1 flying bombs being sent over the Channel was noticeably decreasing as the Allied armies moved into the Netherlands, capturing and destroying the launching sites. However, the German Air Force remained able to air-launch missiles using the Heinkel bombers of III/KG3 which had been moved eastwards to other airfields.

During the night of Saturday 26/Sunday 27 August no fewer than 18 V1s were shot down by Folkestone and Hythe anti-aircraft batteries in less than an hour. But some still got through and at 07.18 a V1 hit Brixton, killing four.

On Monday 28 August, 97 V1 flying bombs were launched from the Netherlands but only four reached London; the fighter cordon shot down 23 and the anti-aircraft guns 65 (Folkestone and Hythe hitting 58 between them), while the remainder struck barrage balloon wires. Some of the V1s contained propaganda leaflets, including a canister found after a crash. There were several instances of propaganda leaflets being dropped along with V1s or shortly before impact, at the end of August; pamphlets were found at Stone and Smarden in Kent. Others came from missiles at Sittingbourne and Dartford the following day. This is believed to have been the first time that the V1s were found to be used for propaganda purposes; the Germans fitted some V1s with a load of pamphlets, along with an explosive device that scattered them just before the V1 reached the end of its journey. (For more information on the leaflets, please see Chapter Eight, November 1944; they were being dropped in greater quantities that month)

Tuesday 29 August: One of the last V1 flying bombs to fall on south-east London glided down in a shallow dive at 14.40 hours and its wing collided with the steeple of Eltham's Parish Church; the subsequent blast killed two and injured 50 more. 200 houses were badly damaged by blast in the town of Lydd, while another V1 hit Otford, killing a married couple and injuring one. The Folkestone batteries shot down 32 V1s, Hythe got another 26.

During the night of 29/30 August, there were seven air-launched flying bombs. Two fell in Essex, one to the west of Aylesbury and two reached London, with no known casualties.

On Wednesday 30 August, the Folkestone guns destroyed ten Divers during the day. By the end of August, the figures had improved dramatically with the use of proximity fuses throughout the gun belt. The gunners shot down 17% of all flying bombs in the area within a week. By the second week, the total was 24%, and by the end of August it was 74%.

During the night of 30/31 August, according to *Defence of the United Kingdom*, written by Basil Collier, twenty-one flying bombs were air-launched towards Gloucester. The city is about 150 miles from the Thames Estuary; this would mean conventional doodlebugs would not have had the range to reach Gloucester from the usual launching zones. They would have needed a range of about 200 miles to hit the city. Between 03.12 and 06.40 there were 20 air-launched divers/V1s, which may allegedly have had Gloucester as a target, but only eight crossed the coast: six fell in Suffolk, two in Essex, with some injuries near Harleston, but no deaths. Presumably the choice of Gloucester was intended to cause alarm; however, those living in Gloucester were blissfully unaware and no V1s came anywhere near the city.

Colonel Wachtel began to evacuate the launching sites on his left flank as Allied troops moved closer and there was a risk of capture. Only the Pas de Calais launch sites were left; by the end of August there was only one battery remaining. This fired its last missiles in the early hours of 1 September; these were the last V1s from France.

On Thursday 31 August there were several waves of V1s launched from across the Channel. Many were hit by the guns and a couple that crashed were found to be carrying propaganda leaflets. With the last two flying bombs from Pas de Calais, one hit Lyminge and one hit Folkestone, damaging more than 400 houses. After that, the one remaining ramp-launched battery left the Pas de Calais. This was the final Heinkel operation of the month, with 228 air-launched sorties flown for the loss of three aircraft, a better return than the previous month.

Some evacuees started to wish to come back to London. However, the government was quick to intervene to prevent this, using excuses like "not enough milk" or the shortage of accommodation. In reality, the government was aware that the V2 campaign was about to begin, and the evacuees could be in serious danger. All the evacuees who had returned to London were sent away again at the government's expense.

Up to nightfall on 1 September, the Allies had dropped 98,000 tons of bombs on targets that were mainly concerned with the flying bomb. More than 74,000 tons had been delivered since mid-June. During that time, probably hundreds of French civilians and slave labourers had been killed by British and American bombs or had been caught smuggling information to the Allies and been killed by German firing squads. Compared with this, the German losses relating to the V1s had been pretty insignificant; even including accidental casualties plus some missing as a result of explosions, the total came to 185, with 256 wounded. 5,000 British civilians had died and 17,000 had been seriously injured. 2,900 Allied airmen had died; 380 of them were from the US Eighth Airforce and 1082 had died from Bomber Command. At this point in the war, the V1 campaign appeared a success for the Germans.

Chapter 5

September 1944: "And Still They Came"

Initially it seemed that the end of the V1 campaign was in sight. The numbers of V1s launched had decreased gradually as August continued. By mid-August Colonel Wachtel's ramp-launching Flak Regiment 155(W) began to evacuate the sites on their left flank to avoid capture by the advancing Allies. This meant only those sites in the Pas de Calais remained effective. As the Allies moved eastwards through France at ever increasing speed, the remaining ramp launched V1 sites had to evacuate with an equivalent urgency. By the end of August, only one battery remained. It fired its last missiles during the early hours of 1 September and promptly decamped.

By the start of September, the effective end of the V1 attacks from France, 8,617 V1s had been ground-launched against the UK. So far about 410 had been air-launched; of these, 300 had been intended for London, 90 for Portsmouth and Southampton, with 20 allegedly directed at Gloucester. Of the air launches against London, only 160 had reached the coast and only 50 had penetrated the defences and reached London. However, the Germans still had more to send, as the month would show.

From 16 July to 5 September, the anti-aircraft guns got a larger proportion of V1s: 1,199 versus the fighters' 847 and the barrage balloons' 176. The grand total was 2,222, 58.6% of the 3,791 targets within range.

There was now a change of strategy. The last flying bomb from the Pas de Calais hit Folkestone at 12.14 on 1 September; it damaged housing and injured 12 people, one seriously. This marked the return of cross-Channel shelling from the German long-range batteries along the French coast, notably at Cap Gris Nez. There was a bombardment for the next two weeks. Ramsgate, Folkestone, Hythe and especially Dover were attacked relentlessly. Dover was hit by 39 shells on the first day, with some deaths. More than 400 houses were damaged in Folkestone. Although the Allied troops in France moved closer to Cap Gris Nez and the RAF bombed the cross-Channel gun sites, the German attacks continued. On September 11, for example, the Folkestone air raid warning lasted 11 hours. This ordeal lasted until 26 September, when Canadian troops attacked and silenced the heavily fortified guns. On the last day, September 26, over 50 shells hit Dover. 40 people were killed and 60 seriously injured. 11 died in Folkestone, two in Ramsgate and one in Hythe.

On 1 September three flying bombs were brought down by fighters; that night, the target may have been shipping in the Channel. The rate of air-launched attacks from III/KG3 then increased. At the start of September, there were 23 air launched sorties from Venlo. On 4/5 September there were 18 air launched sorties, allegedly towards London, Portsmouth, Southampton and Gloucester, though no evidence of the Gloucester attacks could be found. Three V1s came down in East Anglia (Felixstowe, Langham and Dedham), one in Bedfordshire (Eyeworth) and three in Hertfordshire (Kings Walden, Stagenhoe and Ware).

A veteran Luftwaffe bomber pilot, Horst Juventus, who had been posted to III/KG3 for training in air-launch techniques, remarked of the new method: "It was obviously a very indiscriminate weapon and to no good purpose....We flew off from Gilze-Rijen over the North Sea for some distance before igniting the V1's motor and releasing it. The things could be a positive menace as they did not always fly true, and we felt in great danger with the contraption beneath us. I was sure some crews released them as soon as they were out of sight of land in order to be free of them." An interesting perspective, if true, on the accuracy of air launches.

Previously Kent and East Sussex had been given the title of Doodlebug Alley during the first three months of the V1 campaign; V1s that fell short of London tended to land there, and of course those shot down by AA guns and fighters would also be likely to explode there. Starting from September, Essex took over that title, as it became under the direct firing line of the air-launched V1s.

On 2 September the German V2 weapon was declared operational; it would start to arrive in less than a week.

On 6 September, the British government issued a communiqué after a meeting of the Chiefs of the Imperial Staff, saying that the V1 flying bombs to this date had killed 5,817 people; 17,086 had been admitted to hospital with another 22,870 slightly wounded. The statistics for London were: 5,381 killed, 15,777 seriously injured and 18,256 slightly injured. (It is clear from this that although the majority of deaths and injuries were in London, a significant number of V1s had affected other areas in southeast England.)

In other statistics, 8,095 flying bombs had been launched. Of these, 2,337 had reached London, while 3,823 were destroyed by "combined defences". Fighter aircraft had destroyed 1,902, anti-aircraft had accounted for 1,657 and balloon command 264. The communiqué finished by adding that the enemy had been completely driven out of the static launch sites and that a "small-scale" attempt was still being made to launch V1s by aircraft.

The following day, September 7, Duncan Sandys announced: "Except possibly for a few last shots, the Battle of London is over - we have beaten Hitler's secret weapon, the V1, which was to have terrorised Britain into making a negotiated peace." A sweeping statement, but it proved to be untrue. The V1 would continue to be part of the war until the following March.

That morning the first two German V2 rockets were fired against the Allies by German 444 and 485 Mobile Artillery Detachments at 10.30 and 11.40 hours, respectively. They both targeted Paris but crashed immediately after their launch. The third rocket was successful and hit an area in the Parisian suburbs.

Next day it was the UK's turn. On September 8 at 18.43 a fourth V2 hit Staveley Road, Chiswick, killing four (three civilians and one off-duty soldier) and seriously injuring 17, with six houses totally destroyed and a huge crater. There was no warning of its approach as it descended at three times the speed of sound. The only sounds came afterwards – the sonic boom as it broke the sound barrier, the thud of the explosion and finally the noise of the rocket arriving like an express train. The incident was alleged to be a gas main blowing up; there was silence about what had really happened, which continued until the BBC announced the truth more than two months later on 10 November. The second V2 hit near Epping about 16 seconds later and made another large crater. Further V2s arrived on 10 and 12 September, with one falling near Kew. They took a mere four minutes to reach London. The government censored all these incidents for fear of damaging morale. The V2 rocket assault would see a total of 1,115 rockets fall on England (517 fell on London), killing 2,754 people, with 6,523 injured. The assault lasted for a further seven months until March 1945.

Churchill called a meeting shortly afterwards. Herbert Morrison, Minister of Home Security, was one of those attending. He was pressing for more action to be taken against the flying bomb and the V2 as he wanted to minimise the menace to the civilian population. Professor Lindemann set out to prove that the doodlebugs were not such a serious threat as Morrison was implying. He produced some figures which indicated that each doodlebug launched by the enemy was responsible for killing one person, on average. He added that, while this was "unfortunate", the V1 was obviously not really a menace.

Herbert Morrison was extremely angry and disputed the Lindemann figure, saying it was a remote and impersonal view of the situation. He went on to talk about what actually happens when one of these flying bombs explodes. They do not necessarily drop over a wide area. You may get as many as ten in one borough [as happened in Twickenham on 19 June, for example]. One bomb may kill several, not just one, and they wound a considerable number. "They destroy or damage the homes, furniture and possessions of humble people. The hospital services do not merely put the ten corpses from the ten V1s.... into the mortuary; they have the injured from the ten incidents. Civil Defence has a big job, and the local authority has to find accommodation for the bombed-out families. If a factory is hit, there may be only one person killed, but production will be interrupted, and people thrown out of work. Finally, while there will be no real panic, the people, knowing that they are within range of V1s, will be in a state of anxiety. My submission is that the sooner we destroy these flying bomb sites and stores the better, and it is my duty to say so." [Source: *Herbert Morrison, An Autobiography*, 1960]

This excellent description explains in detail why the V1s were such dangerous weapons. What they lacked in accuracy they made up for in overall effect. They could come over by day or night, in any kind of weather, and with little warning as to when and where they would crash and explode. When people describe their experiences of World War Two on the Home Front, it is frequently the doodlebugs which are described as terror weapons, primarily because of the sounds they made (they could be heard approaching for some distance because of their distinctive engines) and the terrifying wait to discover when the engine would stop, followed by the need to find immediate shelter. The sheer unpredictability of the attacks, coupled with the fact that the V1s had no pilot, made many people find them profoundly unnerving.

The evacuees began to return to London, because allegedly the Battle of London was over. Except that it wasn't. The government had to discourage them by alleging there wasn't enough food or accommodation for extra people. The V2 campaign was not formally announced until November, because of censorship; in the meantime, people had to be dissuaded from returning to London, especially as the threats from V1 and V2 alike were continuing.

The V2s continued to come over, albeit in smaller quantities than the V1s. On 12 September, one of the four V2 rockets launched hit the Chrysler vehicle works in Mortlake Road, Kew, including the works air raid shelters. Eight were killed, 14 were wounded, and property damage was significant. Over the next two days, seven more V2s hit the capital, including one in the centre of Walthamstow at 04.55 that left a crater 50ft across and killed six people.

Now that the French launch sites had been overrun, the Luftwaffe re-organised its air-launched bombers and moved them to bases along the German/Danish border. III/KG3 was effectively disbanded and renamed 1/KG53. The new bases included Varrelbusch near Bremen, as well as other airfields on the German/Danish border such as Leck, Schleswig and Eggebek. Because of the changes in location, most air-launched V1s that made it across the coast now landed further north, in Essex, rather than Kent and Sussex as before.

In mid-September the air-launched attacks began again in a line over East Anglia. General Sir Frederick Pile, in charge of the anti-aircraft defences, remarked:

> "After a space of eleven days, the air-launched attacks were renewed, and we found that the enemy was extending their lines of attack over East Anglia to the north of the "Diver Box". Moreover, we heard through intelligence that the Luftwaffe were converting more Staffeln to the role of carrying the flying bombs."

He was having trouble moving the guns into places where they could combat the V1s being launched by aircraft. Between September 16 and 18, 96 static guns were redeployed to the East coast, and a number of anti-aircraft batteries were also moved. He then received the news that the enemy was launching attacks well to the north of the Harwich area, which was a source of concern as he felt resources were limited because of manpower cuts. The anti-aircraft command decided to redeploy all their defences from the South Coast in a strip from the Thames Estuary to Great Yarmouth. It was a huge operation. At that stage, the new gun sites suffered appalling conditions as it was very muddy indeed. There was a controversy over the conditions for the ATS girls working there, who were offered a transfer to more comfortable sites; they declined.

On 16 September, 13 He III bombers of I/KG53 took off from Varrelbusch to launch V1 flying bombs. One bomber crashed and three were shot down over the sea. One V1 hit a water tower at Saffron Walden, at the end of the runway of nearby Debden airfield and caused some alarm among the men of 4th Fighter Group who were billeted nearby. Another came down in Woolwich; one hit Barking, killing 13 and seriously injuring 17, with others falling on Essex villages like Aldham and Wakes Colne.

After that, the air-launched V1s were sent over the North Sea on an almost nightly basis. There was no pattern as to where the air-launched bombs would fall, there had been explosions in Cambridge, Hertfordshire, Suffolk and Essex. Squadron Leader Miroslav Luskin, the commanding officer of the Czech 312 Squadron, wrote later that month:

> "Due to the new developments in enemy activity, it became rather "hot" even at North Weald, where the flying bombs arrived in increasing numbers. One of these V-1 flying bombs was accidently caught in the huge radio mast complex near our airfield and exploded uncomfortably close to the officers' mess accommodation. Surprisingly, that particular one ton of TNT did not cause casualties or damage."

A new technique for gunners to destroy air-launched V1s was developed. As a result, the percentage of kills eventually rose to 82%.

Meanwhile 13 flying bombs landed in Norfolk; they injured 11, but there were no deaths.

On 17 September a German Heinkel bomber was lost when 14 of them took off from Varrelbusch, on a sortie to air-launch flying bombs over the East coast. It had flown into friendly fire and ditched into Lake Braassemermeer in southern Netherlands. Nine of the returning aircraft were also damaged by flak around the Dutch coast. (These messages were all picked up by Ultra intercepts.)

On the next few nights there were increasing numbers of air-launched sorties. There were 14 on the night of 18/19 September after midnight and some V1s got through to the London and Essex area. One hit Maldon, another Manningtree and two fell on Hornchurch. The first hit Crystal Avenue, Hornchurch at 04.33; it killed four and injured 29. Six houses were demolished and 30 seriously damaged. Seven minutes later, at 04.40 another V1 killed eleven (including six from the same family) and injured 38, demolishing a number of houses. More houses were demolished at Mitcham, with another person killed at Norbury. It must have been hard for those involved to believe that the V1 campaign was at an end, given the evidence to the contrary.

A young boy in Great Gardens Road, Gidea Park, gave his account of the second Hornchurch V1 that fell two gardens away from his family. The siren sounded at about 04.30. His father shouted, "Take cover, this one is for us!" He had seen it gliding down. The boy and his uncle hid under the bedclothes. He saw the flash but did not hear the explosion; he must have been knocked unconscious by the house collapsing. When he came to, he found that both he and his uncle were trapped in the wreckage. They had to wait a long time to be rescued; his father, very badly injured, was buried in the rubble nearby. It was six hours before he was rescued, and he was in hospital for three months. The boy's mother was killed instantly by the explosion. The boy was sent to friends in Cornwall for the next three months until his father was fit to leave hospital.

There were 21 air-launched sorties from Varrelbusch on the night of 19/20 September, and a further 13 on the night of 22/23 September. One V1 fell at Little Baddow at 01.45, killing one and injuring two. Another reached Bethnal Green on the first night and damaged property, with others reaching Wandsworth and Hatfield. Two of the V1s recovered were found to carry stencilled six-figure serial numbers; these were thought to be carried specifically on the air-launched bombs.

By now about 1,500 anti-aircraft guns had moved to East Anglia, now nicknamed Buzz Bomb Alley.

On 25 September, four flying bombs penetrated the defences, with some damage to housing; one fell in Chertsey, one in Essex and another at Hessett, near Bury St Edmunds. The following night, one V1 fell at Edmonton, injuring 25, 11 seriously. Three V1s fell in Essex, one in Cambridgeshire, one in Hertfordshire and three in Suffolk. While these were only small numbers, especially when compared to the earlier daily totals in July, they represented a continuing threat. The air-launched V1s were still falling on London, while East Anglia was now receiving the lion's share of those that fell short. There was a backlog of housing requiring repair; the V1s had damaged many thousands of houses and destroyed at least 23,000. Many houses needed further work to make them habitable, despite the first-aid repairs already given to 70,000 of them.

On 28 September III/KG3 flew 20 sorties and lost two of their aircraft. All seven of the bombs that got through the defences fell in the East Anglia region; however, most landed in farmland and there were no injuries.

On the night of 29/30 September more V1s fell in East Anglia, generally without much damage, apart from the one that hit Redbury Farm Cottages, Ardleigh, near Colchester, killing four and injuring five. It demolished nine houses, damaged a further twenty and slightly damaged a pub and two farms. Two others fell in Essex, one in Cambridgeshire, one in Hertfordshire and one in Sussex. The

USAAF supply base at Thorpe Abbotts, home of the 100th Bomb Group ("The Bloody 100th") reported that V1s were flying over the airfield at 150 feet before exploding in the fields surrounding the base.

Records captured by the Allies showed that 177 flying bombs had been launched by the Heinkels during 13 nights of sorties in September 1944. Increasingly the air launches were coming from Northwest Germany; the bombs were travelling at a lower altitude. People in Colchester noted that flying bombs were now a nightly occurrence; Essex was now becoming the new area for Doodlebug Alley.

What would October hold?

Chapter 6

October 1944: "The Wettest Autumn in Living Memory"

By now the V2s were coming over regularly, but because the launch units had moved and had a maximum range of 200 miles, Ipswich and Norwich were the only sizeable places within range at that point. For example, on 3 October, six V2s hit Norfolk. Meanwhile the air-launched V1s continued to arrive, and more resources were devoted to attacking the Heinkel bombers carrying their V1s.

The weather had deteriorated considerably, with October far worse than September. Many felt it was the earliest and wettest autumn in living memory. The accommodation was very poor for anti-aircraft personnel, who had just been moved to new sites, and very muddy ones at that. Any damage to housing was severely felt; leaking roofs and broken windows made life miserable on the Home Front and it was hard to get homes repaired effectively. Windows were re-glazed with a kind of opaque plastic, giving indoor life a kind of Stygian gloom.

Between 5 and 11 October, there was another mini V1 Blitz. 62 V1s were air-launched from the 75 He111s that flew from Varrelbusch, near Bremen. Nine of the bombs hit London. One killed eight people at Wanstead, while six died at Chertsey. All the launches took place during the hours of darkness. It is possible that by now people had stopped using their Anderson shelters as a matter of routine, going out to the garden before the evening alerts began; they may have felt there was less of a threat and as autumn set in the prospect of spending the night in a cold and damp shelter in the garden was less appealing. Many Heinkels and their bombs were destroyed by fighters but the gunners in the new belt north from Clacton to Great Yarmouth had more success. Further south, Dover and Folkestone were both very quiet, with no bombing or doodlebugs, few AA guns and less cross-channel shelling.

On 5 October a V1 near Abbey Field was damaged by AA fire; it struck a tree and exploded at Reed Hall, near Colchester. It was close to an army hut crowded with soldiers and the tree probably saved many lives by deflecting the blast. The Marks Tey area was repeatedly hit by V1s, and a number of air-launched V1s continued to fall in Essex from October onwards. One bomb hit the area near the Queen's Hotel, Colchester, and blew all the windows out.

Three V1s reached London on 6 October, exploding in Surbiton (two deaths), Heston (15 injured) and Edgware (with five killed and 40 injured). The next night saw another 11 air-launched Heinkels take off from Varrelbusch, with more again the following night. Several landed in Essex, one at Little Yeldham and another at Grinstead Green, where blast damaged sixty houses and the village school.

A number of Heinkel bombers carrying V1 flying bombs were shot down on the night of 7/8 October. On October 8, one flying bomb managed to evade the fighters and anti-aircraft guns; instead, it flew into a balloon cable over the village of Fawkham near Gravesend before exploding. It demolished the Mission Hall and the Woodman alehouse, along with several houses; there were no recorded casualties.

On the night of 9/10 October at about 05.00, there was a serious V1 incident at Hornsey between Barrington Road and Park Road. Seventeen people were killed and 54 injured, 20 seriously. Most of the deaths occurred between numbers 61 and 69 Barrington Road, where several neighbouring families were killed outright. Another V1 hit Hatfield at 04.49, killing nine and seriously injuring 30. It caused severe damage to St Audrey's School, damaged council buildings and wrecked many houses in Endymion Road. During the rescue process, an old iron boiler was unearthed. It was later found to contain what is believed to have been a family's life savings, amounting to £500, including four sovereigns which were wrapped in cotton wool. Meanwhile, chickens from bomb-damaged houses had been wandering at will through the back gardens; the birds were apparently quite unaffected by the blast.

The attacks tailed off after 11 October leaving 36 people dead in the south London area. The Divisional Fire Officer at Wanstead where eight were killed recalled:

> "As we toiled, V1s roared across the sky and there came a chorus of "Sieg Heil! Sieg Heil!" from hundreds of German throats in the POW Camp a few hundred yards along the road. How I prayed for one of them to come down smack in the centre of that compound, but my prayer went unanswered, and the bombs flew on to crash in Poplar or Stepney or points west. Casualties were relatively light, and we were able to clear up rather more quickly than usual and make our way home."

Throughout October the bombings continued. Towards the end of the month III/KG3 was reinforced and redesignated 1/KG53.

The air-launched V1s proved hard to counter. In mid-October Air Chief Marshal Hill became Air Officer Commanding-in-Chief, Fighter Command. He was responsible for anti-V1 measures but depended for bombers on Air Chief Marshal Harris. Harris was reluctant to bomb the airfields belonging to the air-launching units, although between 23 September and 7 October the chief German base at Handorf was attacked several times; there were also some raids on Varrelbusch and Zwischenahn. However, little was achieved. It was hard to catch enemy aircraft taking off or landing. The Heinkels were only visible on radar for seven minutes: the time it took each of them to climb to 1500 feet, release its bomb and turn and dive away again. They were very vulnerable while climbing but travelled so slowly at 110 mph that the Mosquitoes attacking them either overshot or stalled. Some out-of-date Beaufighters were brought in to help and some small enhancements were made.

Previously, by early September, the area from the Thames estuary almost to Clacton had been well guarded. However, the V1s were now coming in over Suffolk and Norfolk so the anti-aircraft guns needed to be moved up. There were delays, and the guns were not moved till 13 October. Morale was low.

Intelligence reports suggested that more air-launched V1s were to come into service, possibly for the Midlands and Northwest. More batteries were moved to the East coast, near Bridlington, Louth and the mouth of the Humber. Perhaps fortunately, this would turn out to be just one attack, two months later, but this shows how many potential threats there were at the time.

During the month, Essex continued to be hit by V1s that fell short of London. The Marks Tey area was particularly badly affected, along with other Essex towns and villages such as West Mersea. Air-launched V1s continued to fall in Essex throughout October and November, right up to Christmas. After that the Allied occupation of key bases near the German frontier gave Essex a brief respite.

About a week later on Woodford Road in Wanstead a flying bomb hit an AA rocket installation and injured a number of gunners and ATS girls. The blaze afterwards started a grass fire which nearly set off ammunition on the site.

On 12 October the German 485 Mobile Artillery Detachment, responsible for launching V2 rockets, began their move southwest from Friesland to the Hague in the Netherlands; they arrived ten days later. On the same day, Adolf Hitler ordered that London was to be the only target for V2 rockets in Britain; attacks on continental cities such as Antwerp were to "continue". (See the following chapter on Antwerp for more details)

That night there was a second V1 at Great Dunmow; the first had landed a couple of days before. There were no significant injuries, but it was clear that the air-launched V1s were able to carry out repeat attacks with a degree of accuracy.

At 06.30 on Friday 13 October, a V1 hit Russell Gardens, London N20. Thomas Smith was about 11 years old and was living with his mother, grandfather and eight brothers and sisters; his father was serving in the army. Thomas and his four brothers were lying in bed when they heard the V1 come over; they hid under the bedclothes as they were terrified. It missed the house, but the blast caused the roof and ceilings to collapse; the windows were also blown out. His mother still sent him to school; when he arrived there he was asked about the incident and whether he had been hurt. His leg had been damaged as part of the ceiling had fallen on it; he was sent to the local clinic to get the wound dressed. Perhaps his mother and grandfather needed to concentrate on getting the house habitable, or on arranging alternative accommodation for the family, and felt sending a son to school would be the best way to deal with the situation; the over-used phrase "Keep Calm and Carry On" might have been apt in those circumstances.

Also on 13 October, another V1 flying bomb fell on Southwold in Suffolk. It caused major damage to property but surprisingly no serious injuries to people; in all 357 houses were damaged, while 68 shops, three churches and the fire station were all reported as being victims of the blast. Another hit RAF Raydon near Ipswich; the bomb narrowly missed the bomb dump concealed in woods next to the perimeter; at the time of the incident bombs were being loaded onto transport trucks.

That same day, the Germans realised that now Antwerp was in Allied hands, they were trying to unload military equipment from the harbour there. Hans Kammler, head of the V-weapons programme, was told to switch the emphasis of the V2 attacks from Norfolk to Antwerp in order to destroy the city completely. By then, the first V1s had already fallen on Antwerp. This was the start of a long period of fear and terror for the city and surrounding area, which would last until the following Spring.

On 14 October, a V1 flying bomb landed in a field by the Suffolk village of Hopton. Initially it failed to explode; it then exploded just as a bomb disposal officer was removing one of the fuses. (He is believed to have survived.) Another V1 was shot down near the Red Lion Public House in Steeple Bumpstead, injuring a number of villagers.

At about 01.45 on 15 October, a total of 19 V1 flying bombs were air-launched over the East Anglian coast; nine were shot down. One got through the defensive cordon and came down in London SE15 at 01.50 at the junction of Athenlay Road and Fernholme Road, Nunhead, killing eight residents. The ARP report said:

"It impacted on a row of 2 storey terrace houses of poor construction with 9-inch walls, wood floors and slate roof erected about 60 years ago, at the southern junction of Fernholme and Athenlay roads, causing demolition to 3 houses, damage beyond repair to 19 houses, serious damage to 60 houses. Damage calling for first aid repair to about 500 others within a radius of about 300 yards from the point of impact. Anderson shelters to rear of Fernholme Road badly damaged. There were 8 trapped casualties that had to be rescued."

Later that day, the Home Guard was stood down. It was an indication that the end of the war was getting closer. Nevertheless, the V1s continued to arrive, unpredictable and often causing considerable disruption.

Seventy houses were damaged by a V1 in Kirby-le-Soken in Essex on the night of 17/18 October. This date marked the start of an increase in V1 activity, and more doodlebugs were launched from 18 October onwards. More night fighters were sent up to the East coast to deal with them, but not all V1s could be stopped before they reached London.

October 1944: "The Wettest Autumn in Living Memory"

A V1 hit Edmonton, Lower Fore St/Fairfield Road, on 18 October, killing 12 and seriously injuring 29. It was one of 39 that hit Edmonton in 1944; two more arrived in 1945. Several fell in East Anglia; one killed five in Halton Crescent, Ipswich, including a two-month-old baby girl, and injured 28. (This was one of the worst V1 incidents in East Anglia)

On 22 October, the German 485 Mobile Artillery Detachment, responsible for launching V2 rockets, arrived at the Hague, the Netherlands. It immediately began to set up its equipment for a renewed rocket campaign against London.

In mid-October, Mrs Robert Henrey wrote in her memoirs that she had returned to Highfield, near Sevenoaks to visit friends. She noted that no fewer than 36 people had been killed by enemy action in and around the village in the last three months.

Two people were killed and 69 were injured at 19.40 on the evening of 23/24 October when a V1 flying bomb exploded at the Orsett Road/Derby Road junction in Grays, Essex. It damaged the library and destroyed 2,000 books. Another V1 came down near the town the following day, and another eight civilians were killed by a V1 a couple of nights later.

A V1 flying bomb that had evaded the defences came down on the railway line at Palmers Green Station in Enfield on 26 October, causing the line to be closed for a day and slightly injuring some railway workers. (Some accounts attribute this to a V2, for example: "On 26 October 53 people are injured when a V2 rocket falls in front of a train standing at the platform at Palmers Green. The crater left by the explosion is 60 feet wide and 30 feet deep. Trains are running again after two days". However, most of the firsthand accounts suggest it was a V1.)

Another V1 came down in Milton Court Road, Deptford, killing one, on the night of 28/29 October.

On the last day of October, fifteen people died from V1 attacks during the night and another three died in West Ham just after dawn. The last major incident of the month was at 06.50, when a V1 made a direct hit on the Marie Hotel at Dale Road, Coulsdon; the hotel was used as an old peoples' private hotel. Seventeen of the residents were killed and ten more seriously injured. The hotel was wrecked and many of the 29 guests were trapped in the wreckage. A specially-trained Alsatian dog was sent in to scent out the victims. The proprietor's wife, Mrs Warner, died in hospital the next day and her husband was injured. The Civil Defence worked all day and the following night until everyone had been accounted for. Allegedly this was the biggest number of casualties from a V1 in Croydon.

By the end of October, the anti-aircraft defences stood at 300 static guns, 542 heavy guns, 503 40mm guns and 18 searchlight batteries. The naval frigate HMS Caicos had been fitted out as a floating radar station and a control centre was now employed for duties in the North Sea to help detect the air-launching aircraft. The V1 attacks had been sporadic, but records show that a total of 282 V1 flying bombs had been sent in October, launched by 1/KG53 over 20 nights that month.

Before we continue the general narrative with November 1944, let us examine the events of October and after in Antwerp and Liège.

Chapter 7

October 1944 - March 1945: The V1 Campaign Abroad, Antwerp and Liège

So far, this book has concentrated on the V1 campaign in England from 1944 onwards. However, it would be incomplete without a description of the German Vergeltungswaffe (revenge) attacks in Europe. For the purposes of this chapter, I am extending my remit from the V1 campaign in the UK to cover the use of all V-weapons in Antwerp and surrounding areas so that the range of attacks there can be included. This chapter therefore deals with V2 rockets as well as V1 flying bombs, unlike the rest of this book, as it proved too difficult to separate records of the two types of weapons, both in terms of attacks and in overall casualty records.

The background

After the Normandy landings of Operation Overlord on D-Day, 6 June 1944, the Allies opened a "second front" as they began their advance through France. However, only a week later, the German V-weapons campaign against London began. The first V1 hit the capital on 13 June and by the following weekend the flying bombs were coming over in large numbers. By the start of July, plans for the evacuation of women and children were under way, as casualties began to rise.

Meanwhile, back in France, the Allies were gradually advancing across Normandy to the east. They met with considerable resistance and initially progress was slow. Paris was liberated on 25 August and soon the British-Canadian 21st Army Group had managed to cross the Seine as it was only weakly defended by the Germans. General Montgomery issued a directive on 26 August which instructed his Lieutenant-Generals Crerar (First Canadian Army) and Dempsey (Second British Army) to do three things: to destroy German forces in the Pas de Calais and Flanders, to seize the key port of Antwerp (Belgium) and to press on towards Germany and the Ruhr. The Canadians were to advance along the coast, while the British would advance further inland, roughly on a line from Amiens to Arras.

General Eisenhower, Supreme Commander of Allied Forces in Europe, stressed the importance of taking Antwerp from the Germans. Meanwhile one important benefit of the advance was that the Allies captured the German V1 batteries in the Pas de Calais; these were the original launch sites for the flying bombs against London. While this did not eliminate all V1 attacks entirely, it forced the Germans to retreat and move their ground-launch sites elsewhere. Apart from Dunkirk, the Channel coast as far as the Ghent Canal (which links Ghent to the Scheldt estuary) was cleared of German troops by the end of September.

The British moved into Belgium early in the morning of Sunday 3 September; they intended to advance and liberate Brussels by nightfall. They met some opposition and were frequently uncomfortably close to the fleeing enemy, but they succeeded. The Welsh Guards were first to enter Brussels and were feted by the local population. The Grenadier, Coldstream and Irish Guards, plus the armoured cars of the Household Cavalry were quick to follow them. After heavy fighting the following day, the Guards Armoured Division also went on to seize Louvain.

Meanwhile, 11th Armoured Division were experiencing a less easy journey towards Antwerp as German resistance repeatedly stopped the tanks. Consequently, the Division reached Antwerp on 4 September, a day later. Despite the delay, thanks to close cooperation with the well-organised Belgian resistance movement in the city, the docks of Antwerp fell to the Allies undamaged. They were of key importance; the port was huge and could take up to 1,000 ships.

Between June and August, Allied ground forces had been fighting near the Normandy beaches where the supplies were unloaded. However, once the Allied armies had reached Belgium, the supply lines from the Mulberry Harbour at Arromanches became too long; thousands of trucks had to pick up supplies and ammunition in the Bayeux area and take them hundreds of miles to the front line. Each armoured division needed several hundreds of tons of fuel and ammunition every day to work efficiently; it was a major logistical problem. This was why the Allied armies needed to have access to the port of Antwerp, so that their supply lines could be shortened. However, although Antwerp was now in Allied hands, the inland port could not be used for shipping until the Scheldt estuary was cleared of German troops. This was more complicated than had been anticipated. The German occupiers still controlled the Scheldt River which connected the port of Antwerp to the North Sea. As long as the Germans continued to control the sea approaches and the long winding estuary, access to the port would be impossible to achieve for Allied shipping. The occupation of Antwerp itself was not enough; all the lands surrounding the Scheldt would have to be liberated first.

The Allies had also failed to appreciate the importance of clearing the approaches to the city by seizing the bridges over the Albert Canal. When the British tried to cross a few days later, the bridges were blown up by the retreating Germans, who still had control of South Beveland and Walcheren. Montgomery's 21st Army Group was given the task of clearing the Scheldt Estuary, in order to gain full access to Antwerp. Eisenhower made this his absolute priority on 22 September; the rest of his men had to wait to proceed until the Scheldt area was free of German troops.

On 13 October, Hitler ordered that all V-weapons, both V1 flying bombs and V2 rockets, should now be directed at London and Antwerp exclusively. SS General Hans Kammler was ordered to bombard Antwerp, while defending its harbour against German attacks became a priority for SHAEF. Over the next months, the Belgian city and its port became the area in Europe to suffer most from Hitler's vengeance weapons. It had already undergone two periods of German occupation in less than thirty years: 1914-1918, and again from 28 May 1940 until 3 September 1944. Now it was to suffer the same attacks from V1s and V2s that London had already endured and was continuing to experience.

Jenny A'Court was living there then; she was aged 12 at the time and remembers the attacks on Antwerp vividly. She described the limited air raid precautions available.

Air raid precautions

"We did not have air raid shelters. When the siren alarm went, people would run and shelter in their cellars; some slept in them. If their cellar was not suitable, for example a coal cellar or maybe used for storage, people would go and sleep in a friendly neighbour's cellar. We, and many of our street's neighbours, would go and sleep in the warehouse's cellar in our street which was a new building, hence thought to be stronger than our own older houses. But it was all voluntary, not organised and no provisions were made by the authorities....

"At school, we were taught to get under the stairs ([as they were] often left standing after a hit) or under a table or under a desk; told to crouch, put one hand over the back of our neck and the other hand on the top of our head. Teachers advised parents to make us wear an identity label and carry a whistle."

Sensible advice, until you reflect on its implications and realise that the labels were to identify the children after a raid if they were unable to speak for themselves, and the whistles were to alert rescuers if the casualties were buried in rubble and unable to escape of their own accord.

The start of the attacks: October

On Saturday 7 October the first V2 landed near Antwerp, but there were no casualties. (The first V2 to hit London had landed in Chiswick on 8 September, just under a month before.) On Friday morning, October 13 at 09.45, a V2 landed in the centre of Antwerp and destroyed several buildings; later that day a second rocket hit the city. Thirty-two people died. From then on until the end of the campaign, 175 days later, Antwerp received an average of three V2s a day, striking the city and its suburbs.

The first V1 hit Antwerp on Wednesday October 11 and anti-aircraft defences were put in place by the Allies. Antwerp was not the only target; other cities including Ghent and Brussels were also attacked. While Ghent escaped serious damage at this point, 55 flying bombs hit Brussels within four days, causing considerable damage and alarming the inhabitants.

On 13 October, Hans Kammler, head of the V-weapons programme, ordered his men to change the direction of the V2 rockets and target Antwerp instead of Norfolk. Between 13 and 20 October, 23 rockets were launched towards the harbour, in a bid to prevent the Allies from unloading supplies and equipment there.

The heavy flying bomb bombardment began in the early morning of 21 October, when a number of V1s were launched from Büchel, near Cochem in the Eifel mountains. By that afternoon nine had reached the city, while another four had fallen short and crashed; this pattern of attrition is similar to that for attacks on the UK. A battery at Laufeld to the south carried out a similar attack on 24 October and 79 flying bombs were launched within five days. By the end of the month, 337 flying bombs had been launched, although only 27 hit greater Antwerp and 47 crashed prematurely. Approximately 58 V2s hit the city.

Jenny A'Court wrote:

"I remember the awful growling noise these flying bombs used to make when they came over and the sudden silence that followed when their engine cut out. It was terrifying waiting for the explosion we knew was to come. These flying bombs were mostly aimed at the Antwerp harbour, docks and railway network. Not very accurately, though. We lived in the old part of Antwerp at the time at about 15 mins walk from the river Scheldt. I'll never forget the very first V1 that came down in Antwerp. I was at school in the classroom when there was this almighty loud bang that seemed to have come out of the blue. We all jumped up and recoiled away from the windows. We couldn't make out what it was at first. But later, when we got home, we were told that a bomb had fallen in the Schildestraat near the Museum of Fine Arts in the south of Antwerp. I couldn't understand how a bomb could fly on its own. We all soon learned. There were many more to come and many people died. My younger sister and I made a lucky escape when we were on our way to see my grandma who lived within walking distance from us. A V1 [as we thought] came down behind a large warehouse as we passed it. There was this sudden orange flash with lots of dust bursting out of the building's façade, and my sister and I were suddenly sitting in the middle of the road on our bottoms. I don't know how we landed there. We weren't hurt, but quite puzzled because we hadn't heard a thing. We got up and ran back home. It later appeared that it had been a V2 (which were rockets and were silent). You didn't hear them coming."

Antwerp was harder to defend than London and the Southeast. The Germans were able to use a wider range of launch sites from within Germany, and these in turn were closer to the proposed targets. The flight times were short and the V1s could travel at low altitudes; this meant that aircraft could not be used to intercept the V1s in the same way that they could in England. Instead, anti-aircraft guns were used to shoot them down.

An attack by either V-weapon was a terrifying experience, whether in London or on the Continent. With the V2, if you heard the double bang, you realised you had survived. The death toll for these attacks tended to be large, and there was no time to take evasive action because you had no idea what was coming. Death was a matter of chance; you survived the attack, or you didn't. With the V1, however, the whole experience felt protracted and intensely personal, in Antwerp just as it was in the UK. The approaching doodlebug was often both visible and audible and people reported feeling almost mesmerised by it as they watched it moving towards them. You could see the flying bombs approaching, often several at a time, and hear the distinctive rattling sound of the pulse jet engine getting louder as it came closer; the attack was often in daylight so you might be out in the open, going about your daily business. However, once the engine stopped, you knew that the V1 would glide to earth in a matter of seconds and explode on impact. Both V1s and V2s could come over at any time of the day and night, in any weather conditions. Civilian morale was badly affected. It was a prolonged nightmare and every inhabitant of Antwerp felt at risk, all the more so as the extensive blast damage from both V-weapons became increasingly visible as the campaign continued. You knew what might happen; you could already see the damage from previous attacks.

On 19 October, a V2 rocket hit the Kroonstraat at Borgerhout, killing 44 people and injuring about 100. Less than a week later, on 25 October, Greg Hayward, an RAF airman serving with the 146th Wing, was servicing an aircraft at the airfield at Deurne when he witnessed a V2 attack as the rocket exploded close by. He saw a brilliant crimson flash but had no memory of an explosion. Five airmen died then and a dozen or so were injured, some with life-changing injuries; one member of ground crew serving with 197 Squadron spent more than three years having bone and skin grafts in UK hospitals as a result.

On 28 October at 18.20, at Bontemantelstraat, a V2 hit a densely populated area and completely erased all trace of the street; the houses were never rebuilt. 71 people were killed and 81 were injured, one of the first real massacres of the campaign. Whole families were destroyed; the Benoy family lost their father and mother, their daughter and their granddaughter. The Allies imposed a news blackout so that the Germans could not discover where their V-weapons had hit and thus be able to use that information to improve the precision of subsequent attacks. From the start of the raids, the newspapers stated that they would not mention specific bombings (the same policy as employed in the UK). Antwerp is a compact city, so its inhabitants would usually have seen where the V-weapons had landed and the damage they had caused; however, they were denied any official news about what was happening.

November

On 10 November 1944, the American Brigadier-General C. H. Armstrong arrived in Antwerp to form the "Anti-Flying Bomb Commando Antwerp-X".

This involved stationing US, British and Polish anti-aircraft units (altogether some 22,000 men) in an arc outside the city to provide a barrier against the V1s, along with searchlight and radar units. From October to December the Allies launched numerous sorties against the Hague and the district between the Hague and Leiden in an attempt to discover and destroy the launch sites and storage areas there. Nevertheless, a large number of V-weapons continued to hit Antwerp that month, including six incidents where thirty or more civilians died. On 11 November a V2 fell in Breydelstraat, killing 51 people, including some of the first military casualties. Fifteen Allied soldiers died there, and twelve others died later in hospital. On 16 November at 11.15, a V1 hit a boys' orphanage on Durletstraat, killing 36 children and injuring 125. The next day thirty-two nuns died in the rubble when a V2 hit a convent in Ferdinand Coosemansstraat.

One of the worst incidents occurred on 27 November just after midday, when a V2 hit Teniersplaats, the busiest junction in town and one used by military supply columns. American troops were heading south from the docks to their supply bases near Liège and the British were heading north to the front lines in Holland. The V2 caught an Allied military convoy and hit a water main, flooding the square. A large number of people died; some accounts say 126, others as many as 159 (at least 26 were American and British soldiers) and 309 were injured. The devastation was such that it was impossible to give a reliable estimate of casualties, while many of the eyewitness photographs are too distressing to be reproduced here in any detail. It looked like a vision of hell, with bodies everywhere, some on fire, and blazing vehicles.

During November squadrons of fighter-bombers started to seek out and destroy the launch sites, in the hope of removing the threat at source.

It is extremely difficult to establish accurate figures for the total of V-weapons, but 64 V1s and 126 V2s are said to have hit Antwerp in November; the numbers were clearly rising.

December

By 6 December 2,738 V1s had been launched against continental targets, including Antwerp, and 818 (almost 30%) had crashed prematurely or off target. During December, 52% of all V1s were brought down by anti-aircraft guns, proving the increasing effectiveness of the anti-aircraft units.

However, on Saturday 16 December there was the worst Vengeance weapon incident of the war. A V2 was fired from Hellendoorn (Netherlands) by the SS Werfer Battery 500. At 15.23, the rocket hit the top of the "Rex" cinema in De Keyserlei in Antwerp and exploded on the mezzanine level; the cinema was almost full to capacity with nearly twelve hundred people watching a matinee performance of "The Plainsman". This was a film about "Wild Bill" Hickock starring Gary Cooper and Jean Arthur. The venue was popular with both military and civilians alike, especially on a Saturday afternoon; soldiers off duty were keen to attend, as were parents with their children. The rocket killed 567 people; 296 of the dead were US, British and Canadian soldiers, as were 194 of the injured (there are no definite figures for the civilian injured). Many killed by the blast were found still sitting in their seats, stone dead. Some of the Belgian civilian dead were children who had been taken to the cinema for a Saturday afternoon treat by their parents. Many were very young; more than 70 children died. According to records the youngest child who died was aged 7, while an eight-year-old boy was recorded as attending the cinema with his mother. (They both died.) Around 100 people escaped uninjured via the roof. There were so many dead that the bodies had to be piled up in the zoo for identification; it took almost a week to extricate them all from the rubble. Many of the military dead were buried in Schoonselhof cemetery in Antwerp. Pieter Serrien has put together a list of victims: https://pieterserrien-be.translate.goog/slachtofferlijstcinemarex/. It makes harrowing reading; the sheer scale of the death toll is almost impossible to comprehend, but the names and their lives deserve recording and his work is praiseworthy.

After this incident, all the theatres and cinemas were shut down. No more than 50 people were allowed to gather in any one place. Some who could afford it left the city, and some children were evacuated to the countryside; those who remained felt at times as if they were under siege. By the end of 1944 another 174 V1s had fallen in greater Antwerp (64 in November, 110 in December) along with a large number of V2s (possibly 130, though some accounts suggest as many as 314). More than 1,000 homes had been destroyed and 1,500 civilians killed. In December 52% of V1s launched to attack the city were brought down by the guns. But that still left 48%, or more than fifty.

16 December 1944 was also the day the Ardennes Offensive began. A rain of V1 and V2 missiles fell on Belgium. From then till the end of January 1945, Liège was also constantly bombarded with V1s and the occasional V2. The doodlebugs that fell on Antwerp were mainly launched from a range of places located in the Zutphen-Zwolle-Enschede triangle in the Netherlands. The flying bombs weren't always calibrated accurately and would sometimes drop down too early. As a result, many victims were killed in the Netherlands as well as in the target areas. For example, in the early evening of 16 December, a V1 stalled and hit Eindhoven; it crashed in Woensel. 16 people were killed and more than 60 injured.

As the winter weather worsened, the effects of food rationing began to bite. Belgium relied on food imports, so the Germans had been able to use food rationing as a method of bargaining with the civilian population. Rationing did not guarantee availability. The amount of food allowed was about two thirds of that allowed to German citizens and was one of the lowest in occupied Europe. People grew to rely on fishing or on what could be grown on allotments, plus the black market. Jenny A'Court wrote:

"Food was rationed during the war years…. Every month we were given sheets of ration stamps which had different numbers on them. For instance, number 1 was for bread, number 6 was for sugar, number 10 was meat etc. You tore off the stamps and handed them to the shop keeper with your money. Sometimes people swapped stamps or sold them to each other. The sheets of stamps were distributed and collected in the Antwerp Festival Hall. My Dad knew someone who worked there and was sometimes able to buy a sheet of stamps from him. Nudge-nudge… And, of course, there was the black market. I sometimes think that towards the end of the war, many people would have starved if it had not been for the black market and having the money to pay for it. There was never enough food and what there was of it was of terrible quality. Bread was atrocious and seemed to have been made of potato peel and sawdust. At times Dad was able to get wheat on the black market which he ground in the coffee bean grinder and then made a small loaf. I remember him getting very worried once because an egg cost 13 Belgian francs. Coffee was unobtainable and replaced with roasted barley grains called Kneip. But we got fish, unadulterated herring. Lots of it. We had them fried, or mashed with potatoes, or spread on a sandwich. When word got around that fish had been delivered at the fishmonger's, my mother… would grab her enamelled little bucket, run to the shop and take her place in the queue.

"Meat was unspeakable. I could hardly chew it. It was officially horse meat, but people said it was donkey."

January 1945

Jenny A'Court wrote:

"On New Year's Night, we were "treated" by three V1s coming over: one followed shortly by the other. I was in bed and woken up by the sirens. I was so scared I felt like crying. The worst part always used to be when the engines cut out and the silence that followed, which was just as bad."

The flying bombs and rockets came over soon after midnight. The first was a V2 at twelve minutes past midnight on New Year's Day that fell on Borgerhout; it killed 46 people and wounded 33. The following day twenty V1s hit Antwerp. By the end of January there had been 117 V1s and 155 V2s, although the anti-aircraft guns had managed to bring down 64% of the V1s, a significant improvement on December's 52%. Nevertheless, the city was still being hit by approximately 4 V1s a day; the heavy snow that month made it difficult to organise rescue attempts.

The accuracy of the V1s had never been impressive. However, there was an unexpected problem when the Germans moved their V1 launch ramps back to Germany. Previously nobody had been particularly concerned when there were problems with the launch ramps sited in France. These might be hidden in woodlands, or even placed in village streets; if the V1s misfired, crashing back to earth after take-off or even exploding on the launch ramp, those killed as a result were generally French civilians. Because of this, the high casualty rate was more or less disregarded; safety concerns were not an issue for the Luftwaffe.

Now the Germans began to realise some of the disadvantages once the launch sites were within Germany itself. For example, between 1 and 12 January 1945, no fewer than 124 V1s fell on German troops by accident, causing considerable damage. In just one incident, 4 people were killed and 60 wounded. Definitive figures are hard to establish, but one German account suggests that 22 German civilians were killed, 228 wounded, 24 houses destroyed and 101 damaged on German soil. The doodlebugs did not discriminate. There were also many technical failures, and acquiring fuel remained a problem for both types of V-weapons.

The Germans were very concerned about the possibility of killing their fellow countrymen and so a system of rigorous safety checks was introduced before firing the V1s. This meant that a large percentage, perhaps as many as 200 out of 320 bombs, were declared unserviceable. This in turn meant that the rate of fire of the remainder was slowed down.

With the V2s, the 485 Battery of Group South was equally subject to errors and dogged by technical failures. A lot of the V2 rockets just fell back onto the launching pad or crashed to earth within a mile or two. Previously the rockets had been stored in bunkers and then had their settings tweaked before take-off. Now instead they were exposed to the elements, which made their performance sub-optimal at times.

The Allied fighters were unable to intercept V1s approaching Antwerp and Liège because of the short flight times and the low angle of attack; it was also dangerous because of the large numbers of AA guns in the area. Gradually some of the more enterprising pilots began to attempt to shoot down V1s en route to Antwerp; as early as December 1944, while commanding 123 Wing RAF Typhoon at Gilze-Rijen, Group Captain Desmond Scott was able to shoot down several. In January and February several pilots were able to attack more, three being shot down by a pilot based at Deurne.

February

In February 224 V1s hit Antwerp, along with 59 V2s, bringing the V1 average to its highest point of approximately twelve a day, with many casualties. The guns had managed to bring down 72% of the V1s; by the end of the month, they were deployed in a double gun belt and were increasingly effective against the doodlebugs. The V2s, however, continued to fall at random.

March

The assault gradually tapered off in March, with only 86 V1s and 42 V2s as the launch sites were overrun by the advancing Allied armies. The last flying bomb and rockets to fall on Antwerp were during the period of 27-29 March, roughly the same as in England; accounts differ as to the exact final dates. The V1s were referred to as "little dingbats" but this was anything but an affectionate nickname. You could hear them coming from a long way off and they were normally clearly visible as they flew quite low. They had been a real scourge during January and February but by March the Allied gunners had gained expertise and were able to shoot down most of them.

The first time the press referred to Antwerp as "The City of Sudden Death" occurred in March 1945 in TIME magazine; reporters had spoken to many of the US soldiers working in the port area during the final week of the V-weapon activity. The soldiers described the all-prevailing terror that had affected the city for the past six months. There had also been so much collateral damage. The Allied bombing of the launch facilities caused many casualties in the Netherlands. A notorious example is the attack on the Hague by the RAF at 09.08 on 3 March 1945. The target was the forest in The Hague that the Germans had used as a launch site for V2s. The Allied pilots, however, received the wrong coordinates and the 51 aircraft dropped 67 tonnes of bombs on the Bezuidenhout district, a residential area in the Hague. A total of over 530 people were killed and 344 injured, 3,300 houses were destroyed and almost 50,000 people fled the city.

The port of Antwerp

It wasn't until November, when the last German forces were cleared from the Walcheren peninsula, that the Allies were finally able to take advantage of the port's vast facilities. It took another two weeks for the Royal Navy to clear the mines left in the estuary by the retreating Germans. When the first Allied convoy sailed into Antwerp 7,000 dock workers immediately presented themselves for work in the harbour. Finally, on November 28, 1944, the port of Antwerp was opened. Unloading of supplies began immediately. Since the city had been liberated, it had taken almost three months to secure the harbour. Eventually, almost 9,000 Belgian civilians were working daily in the port unloading equipment and supplies alongside the Allied troops.

The port continued to be attacked throughout this time. The Germans sank one ship, damaged sixteen others and put a dry dock out of action, but this was not a large result for a such a long-drawn-out campaign. On January 8 a V2 hit the harbour and damaged a pier and a freighter. Another ship, Michael de Kovats, was damaged less than a week later by a V2 at Berth 218. However, ships went on delivering supplies for the Allies, despite the many attacks. The docks continued to function, although the V-weapons slowed down the rate of supply. The civilians working there received a bonus in their pay for working in such difficult and dangerous conditions. This form of danger money was called Bibbergeld; this literally translates as "Shivering Money", which highlights the risks the workers ran for continuing to work in the port while the V-weapons were falling.

Statistics

The V-weapon attacks lasted for 175 days and nights. 4,000 V1s and more than 1,700 V2s were launched; 628 V1s and 570 V2s hit the city. (These figures are from http://www.v2rocket.com/start/chapters/antwerp.html. They are a conservative estimate; other accounts talk of as many as 1,600 V2s hitting Antwerp in 6 months.) Only 30% reached their target, but 3,752 civilians were killed and 6,000 injured. 731 Allied soldiers were killed. (Norman Longmate's account talks of the deaths of 3,470 Belgian civilians and 682 Allied servicemen in

Antwerp, with the destruction of 6,400 houses in Greater Antwerp.) Some 3,613 properties were destroyed. 150 V1s fell in the docks area, killing 53 military and 131 civilians, with 500 injured. 150 ships were damaged.

Antwerp received on average about three V2s a day in the city and its suburbs, even more V2s than London. About four V1s a day landed in December and January, with 12 daily in February. The number tapered off in March.

Other accounts suggest the V1s killed 4,683 military and civilians on the Continent, plus 10,075 wounded. Of these, Antwerp sustained the most casualties. Eventually the V weapon attacks on Antwerp came to an end because the German firing crews were forced to retreat due to the Allied advance.

Liège and other cities

Liège was targeted as it was a supply centre for the US First Army and therefore a major US depot. (It had been liberated by the Americans on 8 September 1944) Ghent was also attacked, while Brussels was hit by 55 V1s in 4 days in October. There were sporadic V1 attacks on Liège from early November, starting on the evening of 4/5 November and occurring almost daily from then; some attacks lasted over an hour. On the night of 14/15 November there were three separate bouts, between 17.43 and 04.30 the next day. A British confidential report, Air 40/2656 Flying bombs III KG3, dated 9 December 1944, looked at the bombardment of Liège, 3-27 November; it stated "The V1 is definitely suitable for use as a tactical weapon." Another large-scale attack began at 17.15 on 20 November and continued until 3 December. A V1 hit a trolley bus on 22 November and bounced off it onto a girls' school, killing 36 and injuring many more. The final period was between 16 December 1944 and 31 January 1945, when the last V1 fell on Liège. On 17 December, a V1 hit the fuel depot in Liège and blew up 400,000 gallons of petrol. Guillemins station was hit on 21 December, along with the 28th General Hospital on 26 December (only a wounded German PoW was killed). V2s were also used, but flying bombs were the main weapon. By the end of the attacks on Liège, 92 soldiers had been killed and 336 wounded. 1,062 civilians died in the greater Liège area, with more than 1,818 injured (these figures are taken from a SHAEF report of 1945). 4,300 houses were destroyed and 44,000 damaged in greater Liège.

There were a number of well-documented attacks on other cities. In France there were V2 attacks on Lille, Paris, Tourcoing, Arras and Cambrai. Some are obvious targets; others may have been the result of a V2 falling short. The numbers for V2s on Belgium are larger: Antwerp and Liege, as described above, but also Hasselt, Tournai, Mons and Diest.

This is just an outline of what happened, but anyone reading it can be in no doubt that the V1 and V2 campaign affected Antwerp quite as much as London. The "City of Sudden Death" was a term that could be applied to both cities, and with good reason.

Chapter 8

November 1944: Air Launches and Propaganda

November 1944 started quietly for the UK defences, but the evening of 4/5 November marked the start of another mini V1 Blitz, with 24 Heinkels of 1/KG53 leading an air launched assault. It would be another seven-night Blitz, like the one in October; by the end of it, a dozen Heinkels had failed to return, with half of them hit by the night fighters. During November two extra Gruppen from the same wing (Geschwader) were added to the unit so that ultimately a total of 101 aircraft were available to carry out air launches, albeit not always at the same time. It soon became apparent to the Allies that KG 53 had more resources. In fact, November 1944 was to be the busiest month of the air-launch campaign.

November 4/5 was a cold, overcast and windy night. The attack started just after 19.00 and ended at 19.42. Eleven launches were abortive; six V1s were shot down over sea and five over land. Some losses may have been due to premature detonation of the bombs. V1s fell in Essex and Norfolk. There was one death in Debden, while at Southminster propaganda leaflets were found after a V1 was shot down. These had the headline "V1- those last few shots", a mocking reference to Duncan Sandy's remarks in September about the alleged end to the campaign.

The following night, 5/6 November, was again cloudy and very windy; quite a few air-launched V1s fell to the south of London. The raid began at about 19.20 and ended at 20.30. There were 27 launches; 15 were abortive, three were shot down and nine managed to evade the defences. Seven fell in Sussex, one in Kent and one in Suffolk.

There is a suggestion that at least one of the crews was instructed to carry out attacks on Portsmouth; this had not gone well with most of the previous attempts in June and July. Sirens were heard at about 19.00 on the Isle of Wight as a Heinkel flew down the Channel towards East Sussex. It released a V1 towards Portsmouth but missed the city completely; "it impacted near Littlehampton". (A list of air raids on Littlehampton, dated 10 November 1944, stated proudly that no flying bombs had fallen in the area, "although several have been shot into the sea uncomfortably near") One fell at Frant Place, Sussex, injuring a girl and destroying most of the stained glass in the church nearby. Propaganda leaflets called "The Other Side No. 1" were found close by. Another V1 fell in allotments near Shoreham at 19.37; there were only four or five casualties but five hundred houses were damaged. John Lyne recalled:

> "A Doodlebug exploded by the Green Jacket on the allotments in Eastern Avenue. It was early evening on the 5th of November when we heard a staccato roar gradually getting louder, knowing what it was and not having enough time to get to the shelter we all dived under the table as it got closer, then seemingly overhead the engines cut out and after a few seconds a very large explosion that burst-in our French doors against the curtains, the taped glass was intact but the door latch had sheared off. There was a fair bit of damage to windows in Eastern Avenue. Nearby, neighbours were in their hall when the front door was blown up the stairs by the doodlebug's blast and they spent the next couple of days picking glass out of the banisters with tweezers."

6/7 November saw another attack between 20.10 and 20.40. 27 V1s were launched, but AA fire shot down 17, with no serious damage to property. Nine launches were aborted, so just one flying bomb got through. A pilot who saw a Heinkel about to release its V1 described it as looking like "a sinister black crow".

Officially the general public in Britain remained unaware of the existence of the V2 rocket, although by now it must have been an open secret, especially for those living in London. The concept of a "flying gas main" no longer seemed credible. On 8 November at 14.19, German radio revealed the on-going V2 rocket campaign against Britain to the world for the first time, two months to the day after the first V2 had hit Chiswick. The message was picked up by the BBC shortly afterwards.

There was a one-night gap in the V1 air launches, and then the attacks began again with a single raid from 20.10 to 21.00 on the night of 8/9 November. 32 V1s were launched; 13 were aborted, with AA and fighters accounting for another 12. At 20.45 a V1 hit the junction of Grafton Avenue and Gerrards Avenue, Rochester. It killed eight and seriously wounded 17, with another 30 slightly injured. 575 homes were damaged. Another V1 hit the second largest cinema in England, the Gaumont State Theatre in Holloway, north London, that evening. The cinema's frontage and restaurant were blown out; only the main walls and part of the foyer were left undamaged. Fortunately, nobody was there at the time. It did not reopen until 1958 because of the damage. Another eight V1s came down in Kent, two in Essex, one in Sussex. A V1 was shot down in Palmerston Road, South Stifford, near Grays, Essex; one person was killed and 23 seriously injured.

The following night, 9 November, was extremely windy. There was a double attack from Varrelbusch; the first and heaviest began at 18.45 and ended at 19.15, while the second began at 21.35 and ended at 22.15. There were 29 launches; 11 were abortive and four evaded the defences for the first attack, while three got through on the second. Walthamstow, Kent, East Grinstead and Essex were hit in the first raid, followed by two for Essex and one for Kent on the second raid. One landed at Brentwood at 22.05, killing three and injuring ten in Mount Crescent. The East Grinstead attack included propaganda leaflets, with leaflets called "The Other Side No. 1" found at the site.

On Friday 10 November, the government lifted the ban on reporting rocket attacks on Britain; Prime Minister Winston Churchill announced to Parliament that British cities had been under rocket attack "for the last few weeks". In fact, the attacks had started on 8 September 1944, or more than two months prior to Churchill's announcement; by this date in November over 100 rockets had already landed on London. On the same day, a V2 rocket hit Goulston Street in Stepney, killing 19, seriously injuring 97, and slightly injuring 323; this gives some idea of the potential damage that a V2 could inflict. (Slight injuries are those that would not involve hospital in-patient treatment but might still leave a permanent scar, involving a sprained wrist or ankle, for example. "Slight" was a relative term in World War Two.)

The heaviest air-launched raid took place on the night of 10/11 November. All available KG 53 Heinkels were used. There were two attacks, believed to be from Varrelbusch; the first and heaviest began at 19.22 and finished at 19.48. The second was after midnight, starting at 01.20 and ending at 01.30. Three Heinkels were lost. During the night, 48 flying bombs were launched, of which 15 aborted. The AA gunners shot down 25 of the 33 V1s that came near to the coast; 21 were shot down over the sea but two reached London at Dagenham and Beckenham. There was only one death during the first raid, but some damage to property in both.

After that there was a lull until the night of 13 November, which had a single attack from 17.55 to 18.20. 11 out of 21 bombs were aborted. Only two V1s got through, with no serious damage.

The next night involved a triple V1 attack which coincided with six V2 rockets being fired at London; this meant the capital was under intermittent fire for most of the night. The weather ranged from rain to sleet to snow, along with a 30 mph wind. The first raid was from 18.40 to 19.20, the second from 23.55 to 00.40 and the third from 05.25 to 05.45.

37 V1s were launched; 13 of these aborted and 13 were shot down. Eight made it to London. In the main the first attacks caused damage to property, but the V1 which hit flats at Friern Barnet killed two people and injured another thirty. Several V1s from the second attack reached London. One hit Castlemain Avenue, Croydon; some propaganda leaflets named "The Other Side" were found nearby. Another V1 caused severe damage at St Pancras at 00.30, killing 18 people and injuring 20. At about 01.00 the last of this second series hit Henley Avenue, Sutton, killing 11 (including an entire family in Frogmore Gardens) and injuring 18. Many were hurt when the ceilings of their houses came down. In the final attack, two of the three V1s hit London. One reached Surbiton with some damage to property; a gas main was set on fire. There was similar damage at Bethnal Green; houses were damaged, seven were destroyed and a gas main was set alight.

On 17 November, there was just the one raid, from about 18.50 to 19.30. The weather was still bad, which may have been responsible for the large number of aborted launches: 13 out of 23 launches failed. Three got through. There were two groups of casualties, one at Orsett, Essex, where one person was killed and 16 injured, and another caused by AA fire, which brought a V1 down at Hadleigh, badly damaging the Mission Hall of St Barnabas and killing 11 people. More than 350 properties were damaged and 80 people were rendered homeless.

By 19/20 November, significant losses had reduced the number of serviceable Heinkels to about half the average. (On 20 November KG 53 stated that only 38 machines were in working order.) There were thirteen launchings, with only three aborted; however, most were hit by AA fire off Harwich and Felixstowe. A V1 hit Carlton Colville near Lowestoft at 19.57; two women were killed in Low Farm Drive and 17 injured, with two cottages destroyed. Propaganda leaflets "The Aftermath No. 6" were found nearby. At Brickenden, Herts, at 20.36, there was some damage to houses. Leaflets headed "The Other Side" were found near the site.

By 21 November, the threat from air-launched V1s from Heinkels was becoming an increasing problem as routine patrols did not seem effective; the timing of the attacks was unpredictable and so it was difficult to schedule patrols effectively. It was suggested that an ASV-equipped Wellington should be borrowed to patrol the suspected launch area, along with a Mosquito or Beaufighter to shoot down the Heinkel and V1 once located. One joined the FIDS (Fighter Interception Development Squadron, part of the Night Fighter Development Wing) at RAF Ford for training; it was hoped that the Wellington crew would be ready for operations in early January, less than two months away, under the codename "Operation Vapour".

There was a short gap in attacks, followed by a raid on the night of 22/23 November between 00.45 and 01.05. This took place in poor weather conditions. Only ten V1s were launched; three were aborted and six shot down. There was minor blast damage but no casualties.

The following night, 23/24 November, ten of 16 missiles were shot down. One at Dovercourt left propaganda leaflets scattered about; these were collected by the police. The Suffolk and Essex coastal AA batteries, now in place and fully operational, brought down a total of 25 V1 flying bombs that night. They brought down another 11 the following night. Another Heinkel aircraft of 1/KG53 crashed into the sea, complete with its flying bomb still attached, ten miles off the Dutch coast after it was pursued by a Mosquito.

24/25 November was the final night for air launches this month, as a full moon was approaching. It would be another ten days before the next launch. There was just one raid; the ten launches were between 04.45 to 05.10. Six aborted and the rest were shot down by AA fire. One landed at Great Bentley, Essex, at 04.22, slightly damaging some cottages. Leaflets headed "A splendid decision" were found nearby. Another V1 hit King Henry's Road, Primrose Hill at 05.04. It killed 12 people and seriously injured 29, with extensive damage to property. Walter Leney, a zookeeper at London Zoo, was one of those killed, along with his wife.

On the following day, Saturday 25 November at 12.26, a V2 hit the shopping area at New Cross Woolworths. This was one of the worst V2 disasters. The official death toll was 160 but there were 11 more missing, and more than 120 seriously injured. Like Antwerp, London was being attacked by both V1s and V2s, with devastating consequences. In just two incidents and in a timescale of little more than 24 hours, the V-weapons had killed 180 people in the capital, with 150 injured.

KG 53 records revealed that 316 V1s had been launched on just 13 nights during November. Although many of these were intercepted or crashed, this demonstrates that the threat continued. During the month the V1s developed another role, that of helping the German propaganda campaign. Flying bombs would now deliver "not just death and destruction but propaganda too", as Juliet Gardiner wrote.

Propaganda

It is easy to forget the role of propaganda and censorship in wartime. The requirement to be economical with the truth has been part of a broader strategy for thousands of years. The need to deceive the enemy in order to achieve the element of surprise goes back at least as far as the Trojan wars and is a feature of most campaigns. (Throughout the war the Allied powers dropped an estimated 6 billion leaflets on Western Europe alone.) Noël Coward was seconded to the British propaganda office in Paris earlier in World War Two and gloriously summed up early British propaganda efforts with the lapidary phrase: "If the policy of His Majesty's Government is to bore the Germans to death, I don't think we have time." Both sides used the media as a source of disinformation and tried to deny their opponents accurate information. This might be something as straightforward as imposing news blackouts on breaking news or making sure that descriptions of "deaths by enemy action" were limited in scope and detail, for example allowing only three death notices per incident in newspapers. "Suddenly, last month" might be all the information you could give about the circumstances; you would not be able to mention a specific street or date. That way the Germans could not tell how effective their bombing campaign had been. With the Guards' Chapel, for example, the full story was not released in the newspapers until Monday 10 July, when the blanket ban on identifying locations of incidents was lifted; even the Guardsmen serving abroad did not know what had happened for weeks.

Perhaps predictably, the V1 campaign was also used for propaganda purposes. As far back as 16 June, at the very start of the attacks, the German press talked of the enemy's attempts to destroy the German forces by "unscrupulous barbarity". At 15.00 that day, Hitler's headquarters announced: "Last night and this morning southern England and…London were subjected to a new type of explosive missile." There was a broadcast that evening which alleged that the Germans had been compelled to use the new weapon as a result of British barbarity; it was an act of revenge. Lord Haw-Haw broadcast to Great Britain in English at 22.30 to say that the British were not discussing the battle in Normandy, but rather the new V1. Dense smoke clouds were rumoured to cover Southern England, according to German reconnaissance planes. This was a rather obvious lie, as no reconnaissance planes were available to the Germans at that point. (Lord Haw-Haw was a nickname given to William Joyce, who broadcast Nazi propaganda to the United Kingdom from Germany during the Second World War. The broadcasts opened with "Germany calling, Germany calling", spoken in an affected upper-class English accent and were a popular, if profoundly unreliable, source of information. One of the problems with government attempts at limiting access to information about the progress of the war was that other reports alleging what was "really" happening became almost seductive in their use of detail; people in the UK would listen to the broadcasts in the hope of getting more information. Joyce was executed for high treason after the war, in 1946.)

The German press were anxious to provide some hard news, but in the absence of that they were willing to provide colourful stories for the German public. A few days later reports came that the roads leading from London to the country were full of refugees, most on foot and carrying what possessions they could bring with them. Big Ben was no longer being broadcast "live"; this was true, but only because the British did not want the microphones located nearby to provide clues to explosions occurring in the vicinity. Yes, there was a ban on hosepipes, but this was down to drought, rather than to extensive damage to waterworks. It was alleged that Buckingham Palace had been badly damaged, and King George had fled the country; this was not true.

Similar lies were put out to people in the occupied countries, suggesting life had come to a standstill and seven million Londoners were being forced to camp out. A German "black" transmitter broadcast to North America told its listeners that "not a single building is standing" in parts of London and spoke of an attack on a railway station that had left 3,000-4,000 soldiers killed. These snippets of (dis)information were intended to improve German morale and to suggest that victory was within reach.

By August, the Germans began to use the V1 as, literally, a propaganda vehicle. They fitted some of the V1s with a set of pamphlets and used an explosive device to scatter them as the missile came towards the end of its journey. The propaganda leaflet ejector was at the extreme rear of the V1; it was a cardboard tube about 30 inches long and two and a half inches in diameter. There was a small explosive charge which threw the tube backwards from the tail cone of the flying bomb missile once the V1 had begun its final dive; a second charge then scattered the leaflets, just before the V1 reached the end of its journey, and avoided the possibility that they would be set on fire by the eventual impact of the V1. The individual sheets were intended to drift down and spread over the area. These leaflets are now very rare because most of them were collected by the police; that way there could be no reference to them in the press, so the Germans would not know where they had landed.

The first leaflets known to have reached the UK were found at Stone and Smarden, both in Kent, on 28 August. A canister was also found, which had presumably contained the set. The type of leaflet sent has not been recorded. Some were also found the following day from missiles at Sittingbourne and Dartford. The next lot of leaflets to be found were not sent until significantly later.

Apart from the special leaflets on Christmas Eve, which will be described in more detail later, the others all had the same format, even if the content differed slightly. They consisted of four pages, approximately eight inches by six. Significantly, they were clearly based on a leaflet dropped by Bomber Command on German cities. That had shown Hitler standing smiling in the middle of a large group of corpses, a vivid image that the Germans were keen to use as a template to vilify the Allied war efforts.

The German leaflet found at Stone had a photograph of dead bodies of air raid victims in Berlin, taken after an RAF raid in November 1943. It was captioned: "Do you like that? You may not in a few months' time." The Smarden leaflet was equally unpleasant, showing gruesome photographs from raids on Cologne and Hamburg in June and July 1943. The text tried to blame the British government for the escalation of the air war against civilians, stating the RAF had begun the air war against civilians on May 10, 1940, in Freiburg. (Emphatically not true – the bombing was the result of a Luftwaffe navigational error, as the Germans well knew.)

The Germans continued to use different variations on these leaflets, as well as another one called "The Other Side". This was more detailed, including news, photographs, cartoons and even a crossword called "The V Puzzle", which purported to contain useful advice for the British government. It mentioned the advantages of the

V1, notably that it cost little to build compared with Allied bombers such as the Lancaster. The leaflet was intended to provide a German view of events.

The third set of leaflets was found at Frant, Sussex at 19.45 on 5 November 1944. These were entitled "The Other Side No. 1". One was reproduced in the *News Chronicle* two days later. Herbert Morrison circulated a copy to his colleagues on 11 November. Another raid on East Grinstead at 19.20 hours on 9 November produced another batch; the V1's engine was still running at that point when these were found. A V1 hit Castelmain Avenue, Croydon, just after midnight on the night of 14 November; more "The Other Side" leaflets were found nearby.

The first known copy of No. 2 appeared on 19 November. This time the usual photographs of mutilated corpses were attributed to the Russian war effort. There were at least four more issues of this variant. Another type of leaflet was found near a V1 crash site at Carlton Colville at 19.57 that day; this time it was entitled "The Aftermath No. 6". Further "The Other Side" leaflets were found that day a few minutes later; these were near a crash site at Brickenden at 20.36.

Another set of leaflets appeared on the early morning of 24 November at 05.50 at Dovercourt, after a V1 had been shot down by AA guns. These papers were gathered by the police, who were under instruction to collect up any leaflets they found. Rewards were offered for bringing them in. The Ministry of Home Security was very suspicious about these and sent copies to a bacteriological laboratory; it was thought possible that these might be another way of waging biological warfare. At the start of the war the Germans had mentioned "weapons which cannot be used against us" and so the Government was wary of this new development. At this point it was felt anything might be possible, particularly where V-weapons were involved. There were instructions for the police to send the leaflets to a bacteriological laboratory, to MI5, to the Home Office and to GHQ

Home Forces; they were checked but no trace of contamination was found.

A fourth set fell near Great Bentley, Essex, at 04.22 on the morning of 25 November. These were called "A splendid decision"; they alleged that Hitler only began the bombing of British civilian targets after the RAF had begun bombing the equivalent in Germany.

A few more leaflets appeared on 18 and 23 December. Some "The Other Side No. 2" leaflets appeared near Radlett, just after 04.00 on 18/19 December and still in their brown paper parcel. There were two other types, "Signal" and "POW Post". "Signal" was an airmail version of the Germans' forty-page newspaper, designed for circulation in neutral and occupied countries; the gist was that the Germans would win the war as the Allies would surrender first.

"POW Post" was an unusual idea. Each leaflet was made up of a single sheet, printed on both sides in black and red on white paper. This contained several facsimile letters from prisoners of war (hence the name) whose homes were in the area, with reassuring remarks as a postscript from a British medical officer or the German camp commandant and a note in the top left-hand corner asking the finder to cut out or copy the letters written here and to send them on so that the relatives would receive them as soon as possible. The original letters were allegedly being sent via the Red Cross in the usual channels.

Apparently, the wounded POWs in the camp hospital of Stalag VIIA had been offered the opportunity to send an extra letter via Red Cross channels for Christmas. They were told these would be "going by air". As indeed they were, though not quite as imagined by the writers. One of the more unpleasant propaganda ironies, given that the Germans' choice of transport carried the risk of death for those receiving it if the V1 carrying the leaflets caused casualties when it landed.

The aim of this exercise was to learn where the leaflets fell and so plot the accuracy of the V1's aim. The idea was for the finder to send the letter to the addressee, who would then write to the prisoner (and thus inadvertently to the German censors), saying where the letter had been found. This was quite ingenious, but it failed because the police had orders to collect all and any enemy leaflets. They also had a discreet word with the addressees and warned them not to mention the letters in their reply. An added benefit to the Germans was the suggestion that they treated POWs kindly, a propaganda bonus. At least one letter, intended for someone in Maidstone, was sent on by a passer-by, but as the Post Office was intercepting incoming letters addressed to those named in the leaflets, this too was discovered. The letters were supposed to be genuine (the choice of wording for some cast some doubts), but they did not achieve their propaganda objective, nor did information from any of them get back to KG 53 to inform them of the V1s' accuracy.

Copies of "Signal" and "POW Post" also appeared on 23 December. Some fell near Ightham, near Sevenoaks, at 07.10; others were found at 07.48 near Shinfield, Berkshire.

Different variants of "POW Post" formed part of the notorious Christmas Eve raids around Manchester. (For more details of the raids, see Chapter Ten, which discusses the specific Christmas Eve raids and their locations.) Variants V1, V3, V4, V5 and V6 were found after the V1 attacks, along with a number of copies of "Signal" magazine. It was an ingenious scheme, as indeed was attacking the Manchester area with a large number of air-launched V1s.

The final set of leaflets was found at Gravesend on 14 January 1945. After that the Heinkels no longer had enough fuel to continue their air-launch programme and that particular propaganda war ended.

Chapter 9

December 1944: The First Twenty-three Days

November had been quite a challenging month, with a large number of air-launched V1s, including some nights that involved several sorties. The V2s continued to arrive, to deadly effect. A number of accounts describing V-weapon attacks tended to imply that these incidents were predominantly caused by V2s, perhaps because air-launched V1s were a phenomenon that was little publicised, maybe even not well understood. After all, if the Allies had taken over the launch sites, where could these V1s be coming from? In reality, both types of attack, V1s and V2s, continued to occur during that autumn and into the winter. Although many of the V1s fell short, or were shot down, some continued to get through, causing damage to property at the very least; although the death toll was generally small, it was not insignificant. The allegation that the V1 part of the war had ended seemed to be far from the truth. The threat from air launches was getting worse, not better. "It seemed more than ever like a bitter slog", as one exhausted Londoner remarked ruefully.

By December, people were growing weary. Surely the war must come to an end soon? But there seemed no obvious indication that it would. Rationing continued, and as Christmas began to appear on the horizon, people were trying to plan for a family celebration, perhaps their first for many months. For families where sons and daughters were serving abroad, would they be able to obtain Christmas leave? What about the families where their young children had been evacuated? Could they come home? (Joy Hilder said that after their

Otford V1 the village children were evacuated until just before Christmas.)

Meanwhile the weather was getting colder, which made Anderson shelters even less appealing – mud, cold, and the need to shelter outside in the middle of the night in case of raids, along with the need to take air raid warnings seriously, "just in case". The geographical focus had switched to Essex, a different "doodlebug alley" from the Kent and Sussex of a few months ago. However, if you look at the wide range of places attacked, the chance of being bombed by doodlebugs was at least a possibility anywhere in the Southeast. Should you take a chance and stay in your warm bed? (Assuming of course that your house had an intact roof, windows and ceilings – by no means a given in this sixth winter of the war.) As H.E.Bates said "Winter is not kind to the bombed."

December 1944 saw a continuing assault by air-launched Heinkels, as they carried on sending flying bombs towards London night after night. As can be seen by the analysis of the launches, many V1s fell short or were shot down. However, even one V1 a night offered the potential for damage and disruption. "The bomber will always get through." London remained the focus. By now V2 rockets were hitting London several times a day, along with occasional doodlebugs.

The air launches resumed on the night of 4/5 December with a single attack between 19.00 and 19.30. Eleven V1s were launched, three were aborted and seven were downed over the sea. The remaining V1 fell at East Malling with no casualties.

On the following night, 5/6 December, there were 15 launches between 20.20 and 20.30 but only seven approached the English coast. Of those, three were shot down over the sea. Another three were shot down over rural Essex, causing damage to farm buildings at Takeley. Another hit a wheatfield at Manuden and a third was shot down on grassland at Chignal St James; the explosion caused some damage to Chignal Hall and the Old School House. There was generally some nuisance value when V1s were shot down over land, such as damage to property or farmland, even when there were no injuries. Admittedly there was far less damage than when a V1 made it through the defences to the London area, where the sheer variety of targets available made it almost inevitable that there would be some injury or destruction, however comparatively minor. The surviving first-hand accounts make it plain that the attacks were terrifying; families sheltered together and sometimes died together. On this occasion a V1 exploded in trees at Oak Hill, Walthamstow, at 20.32. Ironically this was just when the War Damage Architect was addressing a meeting of local residents in the Lloyd Park Pavilion; he had just given the figures of up-to-date damage. There were no serious injuries but over 500 houses were damaged.

Between 18.30 and 18.55 on 7 December there were over 20 V1 launches. However, eight aborted and nine were shot down over the sea; another three were shot down over land. One fell at East Horndon, setting fire to haystacks and causing slight damage; another exploded in a field at Foulness Island and a third came down on Mersea Island, damaging some wooden bungalows and causing some slight casualties. There was then a gap for a couple of nights.

On the evening of 10 December, a stray V1 hit Chelmondiston in Suffolk after being hit by AA fire. It fell on Myrtle Cottage near the church at 18.50. The house was blown to pieces, killing one and injuring twenty, while the church of St Andrew was almost destroyed and only the tower and part of the chancel were left standing; it had to be rebuilt after the war, and was the only church destroyed by enemy action in Suffolk during World War Two. The school was also beyond repair and the authorities were forced to send the pupils to Shotley school instead for some time. Several houses in the village were also damaged.

On the next evening fourteen Heinkels launched V1s, but only seven doodlebugs approached the coast as seven aborted; two were shot down by naval AA guns over the sea and the remaining five were hit by AA fire. One got as far as London before it was hit, then fell in Fairfax Road, Tottenham, at 18.55. 13 people died, and 88 were injured, 30 of them seriously; the bomb affected just over one hundred people, a remarkably high number. Seven houses had to be destroyed and another eight were seriously damaged. An eyewitness described the tremendous pressure when the V1 hit; he was in a Morrison shelter with his father, mother, grandmother and brother. All of them survived, but many others were trapped in the wreckage, with trained dogs brought in to search for people. A gas main burst, so there was danger from fire as well. David Norman wrote:

> "We lived at number 88 (the bomb fell on the even numbered side not the odd) only 4 or 5 houses away from impact and the whole house came down on us. Luckily when we heard the bomb we dived into our Morrison shelter (like a big metal table with wire mesh around each side). It saved our lives. We were finally dug out by friends coughing and spluttering in the plaster dust. In true Brit tradition there was a van already in the street serving cups of tea by the time we were rescued."

On 12 December another 14 Heinkels launched their V1s between 20.22 and 21.08; these came from Schleswig, Lock and Eggebek, just to the south of the German/Danish border. There were a number of launch problems; one V1 was released over the city of Schleswig, with no recorded casualties, and at least two others failed to start on release. Half the launches were abortive but four got through, causing damage to property but no fatalities.

The next night there was a raid between 19.05 and 19.40. Fourteen V1s were launched, of which three got through, with damage to property in Essex, Hertfordshire and Suffolk but no significant casualties.

The official records for KG 53 show that between 1 and 13 Dec, on 6 nights, 90 V1s were launched.

Two US fighter pilots, Lieutenant Norman "Bud" Fortier (1922-2005) and his friend Lieutenant James Duffy (1918-1994), both of the 355th Fighter Group, were based at Steeple Morden, near Royston. They had a two-day leave in London and arrived at Piccadilly just before noon; they checked in at the officers' hotel on Jermyn Street and then headed for "Rainbow Corner" on Shaftesbury Avenue for lunch. As they headed towards Regent Street, they heard the distinctive sound of a doodlebug engine. They looked up and could see the V1 clearly, less than a thousand feet above; it was almost overhead. Everyone stopped and stared; shortly afterwards, the noise stopped and the V1 began to lose height. It was clearly going to crash in the very near future. There was nowhere nearby to take shelter, so they both pressed themselves against the wall, along with many other people. The doodlebug kept on going, losing height rapidly; it was only 200 feet up when it passed overhead, and it eventually crashed with an ear-splitting roar about three blocks away. Almost immediately everything started again, both traffic and pedestrians. As the airmen moved away from the wall, an elderly woman passed them, muttering to herself, "Bloody nuisance, these buzz bombs!" The story comes from "Bud" Fortier's autobiography. It is an example of how flying bombs could pose a threat at any time; this V1 had got through to Central London despite all the defences. Even on leave, servicemen could still be at risk, by day and by night.

There was a gap of several nights before the next raids in the early hours of 18 December, a week before Christmas. There were two attacks from separate launch zones. The first lasted from 03.45 to 04.35, then the second after a short gap lasted from 05.30 to about 06.55. This was launched not far from the Norfolk coast so was more easily observable by radar. Forty-five flying bombs were launched; 16 of these aborted. Seven crews reported unsuccessful launches. Fifteen were shot down over the sea and five over land. Four V1s were later shot down by Tempests and the coastal guns got all but three of the remainder. The final three made it to Skeffington, Radlett and Stanmore respectively, with only a couple of casualties; the attack on Skeffington was the only V-weapon to reach Leicestershire. The first attack caused damage to buildings. At Radlett more leaflets were found near Kendal Hall, still wrapped in brown paper and headed "The Other Side No. 2"; these were the first known copies of that type. The second raid again caused damage to property. The sorties were not without incident; a couple of Heinkels fell directly into the sea and three crews reported friendly fire.

Early on 23 December there was a token raid from 06.45 to 07.45. There were eight launches, of which three were abortive. It was not a successful mission; allegedly three aircraft were damaged while taxiing at Schleswig, another aircraft crashed due to pilot error, yet another crashed on take-off and blocked the runway for 20 minutes …the list of problems went on. At least two Heinkels were fired on from the sea by German craft. At Ightham five people were injured and 70 houses were damaged. Propaganda leaflets entitled "Signal" and "V1 POW Post" were found at Ightham at 07.10. Another V1 landed at Shinfield, near Reading; again "Signal" and "POW Post" leaflets were found at 07.58. The mission was described as "poor". Not a good omen for what was to come.

Chapter 10

December 1944: The Christmas Eve Raid

It was approaching the sixth Christmas of the war, and by now people were becoming weary. They had hoped that after D-Day and with the start of the second front, there would be a decisive victory before the end of the year. However, Caen had not been taken by British and Canadian troops till 18 July, over a month after the Normandy landings. In September, Operation Market Garden was intended to establish a bridgehead over the Rhine and create an Allied invasion route into Northern Germany. The hope was that this might end the war by Christmas. However, the Allied Airborne Army landings at Arnhem and elsewhere failed, after a nine-day battle with heavy losses.

Shortly before Christmas, on 16 December, news came of the start of the German counter-offensive in the Ardennes, often known as the Battle of the Bulge. It was the last major German campaign of the war on the Western Front, with heavy casualties, and continued until 28 January. It became clear that, once more, the war would not be over until sometime in the New Year at the earliest.

Meanwhile the weather in Britain was increasingly grim, with fog and drizzle followed by snow in December. It was a bitterly cold winter; it would be the coldest Christmas for half a century. All those whose homes had been damaged by bombs found life was made even more difficult by the freezing weather; every draught, missing tile and cracked windowpane made the house even colder. Families started to prepare for Christmas, with relatives gathering and sons and daughters in the Services hoping to return to the family home to spend leave there. Despite all the shortages, people tried to plan for a celebratory meal. Often it was a triumph of ingenuity over rationing, for example the Christmas meal known as "murkey" (mock turkey), "without a feather in sight". The ingredients were sausage meat, breadcrumbs, bacon, herbs, onion, apples and parsnips, probably not in that order; the mixture was made into the shape of a turkey, with the parsnips placed to resemble turkey legs, and then the whole thing was covered in bacon rashers. It would have been more of an onion and apple mixture than anything else, and largely vegetarian, but probably quite tasty.

Doreen Smith (later Bull) was 14 at Christmas 1944 and was living in Wembley, north-west London; she contacted me to tell me more about what was available at that time.

She wrote:

"Usually, you had to register with a butcher, a grocer and a greengrocer. You couldn't just go anywhere [to buy meat] and of course only chicken was usually available. We grew vegetables [in the back garden]. [The motto was] "dig for victory." If people did not have a back garden where they were living, then they might be able to rent an allotment.

"During the year, my Mum would put any dried fruit and flour, along with tinned fruit if she could get it, in the sideboard, along with chocolate and sweets. We had 2-4 ounces of sweet rations a week; the amount fluctuated, starting on 26 July 1942. I don't remember having a Christmas cake, but it would usually be a fruit cake that Mum had made. More cake than fruit. We did have apple and cooking apple trees in the garden. (There were no bananas or oranges as they would have had to be imported.) Maybe if you were lucky a pear [from the greengrocer].

"Cooked meat was hard to get, as was tinned salmon, but Mum usually had a small tin of salmon which she had saved for a special occasion. You might be able to get celery and tomatoes, while winkles, cockles and mussels were around. Fish was scarce, though eels were plentiful.

"There were no Christmas trees. You made your own decorations or used what you had had before the war. You could create Christmas decorations by dipping pieces of holly in a strong solution of Epsom salts, so they would look frosted. You might also make paper chains.

"Bread was around but Lord knows what they put into it. Sandwiches might be paste or jam. As you know our merchant ships took a bad loss as Hitler wanted to starve us. People who had chickens, like Dad's parents, had to register with them [the authorities] to get your eggs if you were lucky. We did have food bins in the street to feed the pigs on the farms, but I can't remember having joints of meat. One chop. Sausages (no idea what went in them either). A lot of rabbit. It wasn't rationed and when baked it did taste like chicken. For Christmas, if Mum could not get a chicken, then it was rabbit."

If you didn't have access to eggs from a local chicken, you might be able to get an egg via your ration book allocation and your grocer. By now dried eggs were available, usually in tins. They were an acquired taste but could be relatively palatable in dishes such as scrambled egg.

Rations were increased at Christmas. Children aged six and over got an extra half pound of sweets for the four-week rationing period. All holders of ration books were allocated an extra half pound of margarine and sugar, plus extra dried fruits, while the over 70s would get an additional ounce of tea weekly. The meat ration increased from 1 shilling and 2 pence to 1 shilling and 10 pence for the week before Christmas.

The Christmas Eve Raid

Nobody was expecting the Germans' next move. It was a last desperate attempt to cause alarm and despondency by using V1s "out of area" and at a time when the Allies would not be prepared. The day before Christmas, they made a concerted attempt to evade the East Coast defences (just as General Pile had feared) by aiming an attack further north, trying for an area which had not previously been touched by flying bombs. They calculated that vigilance was likely to be at its lowest in the early hours of the morning and set about attacking in force.

In the early hours of Christmas Eve, Sunday 24 December 1944, the Germans launched a V1 attack on a new area; almost the whole strength of Kampfgruppe 53 took to the air. Up to 45 Heinkels took off, one by one; all carried V1s under their starboard wings and travelled almost due North to carry out their launches. These took place over a period of about an hour, between 05.00 and 06.00 and each missile took on average about 30 minutes to complete its flight once the launch had taken place.

The air launch procedure was very dangerous for the pilot and crew. It was much harder to manoeuvre the aircraft once it was carrying the extra weight of the V1; in essence the aircraft itself became a flying bomb. The additional weight made it harder for the Heinkel to gain height; once it was over the sea it had to fly almost at wave height to try to evade British radar. Then to establish launch height it had to climb. During the launch process, the pilot had to fly fully illuminated; when he launched his doodlebug, it was as if someone had turned a spotlight on him. For the two minutes of the launch process, he was a very visible target for any British fighter who cared to attack him. Some did. After that he could dive away and head for home. During the launch process, the pilot would also have to dodge any other doodlebugs that might have fallen off other Heinkels ahead of him (and that was far from a rare occurrence). More than 40 V1s were fired that Christmas Eve but only 31 made landfall; the rest fell short. Several RAF coastal radar stations were able to identify the "blips" of the approaching Heinkels, followed by the "blips" of the flying bombs as they separated and headed for the coast, while the Heinkels headed back to base. Some trawler crews also described seeing the launchings as these were so well illuminated.

One Heinkel was brought down by a night-fighter, but almost all the others managed to launch their missiles just off the East coast, roughly between Skegness in Lincolnshire and Bridlington in Yorkshire; this was a front of more than seventy miles. Some missiles, possibly as many as fourteen, crashed almost at once into the sea, while the defences around the Humber engaged seven V1s unsuccessfully. In one case near Mundesley, the engine had already started to fire up on a V1, but the bomb failed to separate from its parent aircraft. They then dived together into the North Sea, united to the last.

In all 31 V1s made landfall and reached the target area that morning, between 05.28 and 06.25. Just as they had taken off one by one from beneath their Heinkels, they reached land in the same sequence. At the last minute, one V1 crashed into the mud of the river Humber, with its motor still running.

Despite the Luftwaffe's suggestion that all these weapons were intended for Manchester, the V1s that reached England were spread between Spennymoor/Tudhoe to the north and Woodford to the south. The range was comparatively accurate, but the direction perhaps less so. None actually hit central Manchester, although fifteen bombs fell within the Manchester area. Many of the 31 V1s fell in rural areas and landed harmlessly in fields. However, this wasn't always the case. The total death toll came to about fifty people, while over 100 were seriously injured. Some of them remained in hospital until well into the New Year.

Let us examine the final destinations of the V1s in more detail, county by county. It is worth noting that many of the missiles carried small packets of leaflets. These were of two types, as described in the November chapter on propaganda. One type was a miniature version of the German magazine "Signal". This was printed in English in an 8x6 inch format. The second was printed in single sheets, printed on both sides in black and red on white paper, headed "V1 POW POST". It contained three or four letters, both printed and reproduced in facsimile.

No fewer than 6 V1s reached Cheshire, in the north-west. The most westerly V1 at Kelsall included some "POW Post" leaflets as part of its payload; it caused minor damage but no casualties. This was the most westerly of the V1s. At Macclesfield Forest, near Tegg's Nose Country Park, the explosion caused serious injury to one person and demolished a hen house at Crooked Lane Farm. Later two young brothers found some propaganda leaflets and magazines at Five Ashes, presumably dropped from the V1, and buried them close to the roots of a tree in a nearby field. These were never dug up again. At Ollerton a farm worker received slight injuries; two days later leaflets from the V1 were found in a hedge, still in their wrapping. At Adswood, near Stockport, a V1 landed in a garden in Garners Lane at 05.30; two men were injured and later died at Stepping Hill Hospital. Joseph Briscoe, aged 75, died later that same day, while William Henry Etchells, aged 62, died of his injuries on 5 January 1945. (His wife and daughter survived.) Four people were seriously injured and nineteen slightly injured, including fourteen children.

At Westwood Farm, a dairy farm near Hyde, two died: a grandmother, Elizabeth Greenwood, aged 70, who was visiting her daughter Eveline and son-in-law Edwin Foulkes for Christmas, and her sixteen-year-old grandson, Gordon Foulkes. They were sleeping at the back of the farmhouse, along with Gordon's thirteen-year-old sister Betty. Betty was sharing a bed with her grandmother, which shielded her from some of the blast. Edwin, a dairy farmer, was already awake at 06.25 and preparing to do the morning milking when he heard the doodlebug approaching. Betty and her parents were severely injured by the blast; her mother and father were in the bedroom nearest the explosion. Eveline suffered permanent eye damage and Edwin was left with a scar; for some time, Betty continued to discover pieces of glass emerging from under her skin as a result of the explosion. The farm was wrecked and a nearby pub was damaged. Six cattle were killed or fatally injured, and a pony used for the milk round had to be destroyed. After Edwin came out of hospital, he no longer wanted to farm; instead, he built a house on the site of Westwood Farm.

One V1 reached Newport, Shropshire, but caused no casualties. It left copies of "POW Post" and "Signal" magazine scattered about.

Eight V1s hit Lancashire and a number of people were killed.

Oldham, Abbey Hills Road, was by far the worst incident of the Christmas Eve attacks. The town had suffered a previous heavy raid on the night of 12/13 October 1941, lasting two hours and with as many as 30 bombs; 27 people died then. Nevertheless, nobody was expecting another raid three years later, least of all one carried out by a V1 just before Christmas.

The final casualty figures for Oldham were not published until 21 April 1945 so there are some discrepancies; several records suggest 27 were killed and 49 seriously injured. I have found 32 named victims, possibly more, with a further seven unidentified, while another account suggests the attack seriously injured 67 people and damaged hundreds of homes. (I have since found a reference in *Luftwaffe Over Manchester*, p 49, by Peter J. C. Smith where he states, "No trace of one woman was ever found and at the coroner's enquiry it was concluded that she was a victim of "enemy action" and must be counted amongst the dead." Hence the death toll may be as high as forty.)

A local paper spoke of 53 people being injured, with 38 being treated at the Oldham Royal Infirmary. It is unlikely that the full figures will now be established. The dead ranged in age from young children (the youngest was 19 months old) to a woman of 79. There is a plaque commemorating the incident, placed in 2014 outside 145 Abbey Hills Road; however, the casualties are not named on this. Over 1,000 houses were damaged by the blast.

The air raid siren sounded in Oldham just before 05.30 on Sunday, Christmas Eve. Several first-hand accounts mention hearing the siren, but nobody was expecting a doodlebug attack in that area. Many families had already begun to gather for Christmas, so there were more people around than would normally be the case. Sons and daughters in the services who had been granted Christmas leave had returned to their parents' homes; relatives wanted to join their extended families to celebrate the end of the year. The casualty lists reveal how close-knit the families were; the 1939 Register makes it plain that many of the families involved had been living in the same houses six years before, with relatives nearby, and would have known their neighbours well. A bundle of propaganda leaflets, "POW Post", was released by the doodlebug as it began to descend; these were found in Lees Cemetery, less than a mile due east of Abbey Hills Road.

At 05.50 the V1 exploded along the south side of Abbey Hills Road; it made a direct hit on number 145 and destroyed thirty-five houses. Over a thousand more in the area were damaged from the blast. The explosion left items like bedding festooned among the branches of the trees like some strange type of decoration. Presents and Christmas trees were scattered among the rubble. Where tables remained intact, the Christmas food already laid out on them was covered with plaster from collapsed walls and ceilings. There was dust everywhere, along with the smell of gas from broken domestic gas pipes. Many people were trapped in the rubble and were crying for help. Within 10 minutes a control centre had opened and was dealing with reports detailing the incident. By 06.10 the first ambulances had arrived and before 09.00 an incident inquiry point had been set up by the WVS (Women's Voluntary Service). It handled 450 inquiries in the first two days alone.

Three members of the Holmes /Broadbent families were killed at number 145. Hannah Mary Holmes, aged 62, was one of the casualties at first unidentified. Her brother William also died, aged 49; his body was eventually found on 26 December and was identified by their elder brother Harry. Louisa Holmes Broadbent, aged 47, also died there; she was their niece, the daughter of Elizabeth Holmes (Hannah and William's elder sister who married William Broadbent).

On the previous day, Charles and Hilda Kirkland had held a wedding party for his younger sister Ethel at 151 Abbey Hills Road; she had married Robert Molden. The house was full of visiting family; at least twelve people had been staying there overnight, with a number of relatives on Hilda's Hutton side of the family coming from Chesterfield for the festivities. Four of them died during the incident and one died later. Fortunately, the bride and groom had gone to stay at a house a short distance away.

Ernest Hutton was the younger brother of Hilda Kirkland; he had come from Chesterfield with his nineteen-month-old son Malcolm to attend the wedding. Malcolm became the youngest victim of the Oldham V1 incident and died at the house; his uncle Charles Kirkland reported the death. Malcolm's father Ernest remained gravely injured in hospital and died on 29 December at the Royal Infirmary; his brother-in-law, William Lowe, of 70 Abbey Hills Road, was present at the death.

David Brown Kirkland, son of Ernest Arthur Kirkland and nephew of Ernest Hutton, was born in October 1929; he was named Brown after his mother's maiden surname. She was born Eliza Ann Brown; she died shortly after his birth, and he was brought up in Chesterfield by his father and one of his mother's relatives. He died at number 151, aged 15; at the time he was sharing a bed with his older cousin

Kenneth Kirkland, aged 17 and son of Charles and Hilda, who survived the bombing. David's father Ernest reported his death.

Two young girls also died at number 151; both were part of the wedding party. Hilary Kathleen Hardwick, aged four, was from Chesterfield; her mother Freda Mary née Kirkland was the sister of Charles Kirkland. Maureen Colls, aged ten, was from London; she may have been an evacuee.

Many survivors suffered life-changing injuries. Doreen Kirkland, then aged eight, was the daughter of Charles and Hilda Kirkland and the sister of Kenneth; she later gave a vivid account of the bombing. She lost three cousins and an uncle in the incident, as well as several local friends. She was buried alive in the wreckage and was afterwards in hospital for months. Her mother Hilda was the worst injured of all the survivors; she was left partially paralysed, unable to use her legs and an arm. After Doreen left school, she became her mother's full-time carer.

The Kirklands' next-door neighbours, the Roe family (George Denton Roe, aged 51, his wife Alice, aged 44 and their son Norman, aged 17) died at 149 Abbey Hills Road. Norman's body was not found until 27 December and the death was reported by his brother William.

Across the road two young sons also died. Ordinary Seaman Norman Travis, aged 19 and serving on HMS Victory, was on Christmas leave from the Navy. His younger brother Keith was 17 and a sea cadet. Both died at the family home at 146 Abbey Hills Road and were buried at Hollinwood Cemetery. Their mother and sister were injured and taken to Oldham Royal Infirmary; they survived.

Irene and Stanley Jones, a young couple in their twenties, died together at 143 Abbey Hills Road, next door to the house that took the brunt of the explosion. Joseph Lundy, aged 54, died at 140 Abbey Hills Road, along with his mother-in-law, Lucy Ann Thornton, aged 79. Florence Hilton, aged 60, died nearby at 141 Abbey Hills Road; she had taken shelter in the basement, and it collapsed.

Three members of the Ashton family died next door: two cousins, Alan, aged 2, George, aged 12, and Mary Ellen Ashton, aged 49, of 139 Abbey Hills Road. They were initially buried in Hollinwood Cemetery on 29 December in a communal grave, along with the remains of seven unidentified persons. They were later exhumed in 1954 and buried in Oldham (Greenacres) Cemetery; the remains of the seven unidentified persons were then cremated and placed in a casket at the foot of the Ashton grave.

Joan Hobbs (née Chadderton, 1923-2014, who was living with her parents at 65 Abbey Hills Road) left an account of the raid. Her son, Jeffrey Hobbs, wrote: "Mum was in bed when the flying bomb landed. Her mother was in the other bedroom. Mum heard the V1 engine cut out, knew what was going to happen and called out to her mother to take cover. Grandma refused to get out of bed and said something rude about Adolf Hitler. They were unhurt but windows were smashed and furniture damaged. We still have a writing desk which was damaged and repaired afterwards."

Joan later went out to help with the rescue effort. She wrote about a "young woman pulled out of the rubble wearing only [a] chemise or vest. Bitter cold – we pulled her out of [the] totally demolished house and took her to [the] house opposite, they were neighbours and were taking in casualties." Joan's father, William Chadderton, was an air raid warden and was out on duty with a colleague, Albert Barker. "The bomb fell behind them as they patrolled. They flung themselves on the floor; when the bomb had exploded, they got up again, turned round and the other man shouted to my dad: "Oh God, Will, it's my house!" They turned back and ran to the damage, where his colleague found his young wife alive but [his] two small children dead. Such a tragedy."

Peter Farrand described how his uncle Albert Barker was an ARP warden in Oldham and lived with his wife at 136 Abbey Hills Road, with Peter's two young cousins, Clifford and Kathleen, aged nine and three. Albert was on ARP duty after the explosion when he realised his own house had just been hit. He went on to discover his two children dead in the ruins; he had to break the news to his sister, Peter's mother, on Christmas morning and for many years the family felt unable to celebrate Christmas. The two children were buried in the same coffin at Oldham (Greenacres) Cemetery.

Charles Arthur Jackson, a retired policeman, aged 51 and his wife Eva, aged 52, died at 132 Abbey Hills Road while sisters Clara, aged 69, and Emily Hardy, aged 65, died at 128 Abbey Hills Road. In 1939 they were living there with their adopted sister Dorothea, but she survived the bombing.

Other victims died later. Some can be linked directly to the incident, while the circumstances for others are less certain. Joseph Cocker, aged 52, had been injured at Abbey Hills Road and died just over a month later on 27 January at Boundary Park General Hospital. Edmund Wilcock, aged 54 and an ARP worker, was injured at Abbey Hills Road and died on 8 January; his death from rupture of the heart was thought to be hastened by his rescue party duties.

Samuel Wolfenden Bradbury, aged 69, died from injuries received when his house at 129 Abbey Hills Road was bombed; he died on 25 February 1945 at his nephew's house. He is recognised by CWGC as one of the civilian war dead. His next-door neighbour, James Greaves Wilde aged 79, of 131 Abbey Hills Road, died on 12 January 1945. James's death is not recorded by CWGC as a war casualty but seems likely in terms of location and timing. Eveline Martin, aged 32, of 201 Abbey Hills Road, died on 30 December 1944 and was buried on 3 January 1945; it seems probable that she was another victim, although there is no mention of death by enemy action on her burial record in Chadderton Cemetery. Sarah Ann Brown, aged 67, of 306 Abbey Hills Road was buried on 29 December at Chadderton Cemetery and is another possible victim.

The full story of the casualties may never be known, but it is clear that many families and neighbours were involved, and the bombing would be remembered by many from that area. Possibly as many as a hundred people were killed or injured. This was by far the worst incident of the Christmas Eve raid.

To return to the other Lancashire incidents:

A V1 fell in Parrs Wood, Didsbury at 05.30; it was the only one to hit the Manchester civil defence area, but there were no casualties and it exploded in a field of sprouts. (Perhaps not ideal, given the timing: had the sprouts been earmarked for Christmas Day?)

In Worsley, a V1 hit 18 Woodstock Drive at 05.30. It killed a small boy, Brian Walter Ainsbury, in the house next door. He was aged 4 and was sleeping downstairs that night because he was recovering from measles. Five adults were injured including Brian's parents and were taken to Hope Hospital at Salford. Two houses were demolished, and two others were severely damaged. The doodlebug came down three miles west of the city centre. As it came over the city, London evacuee children at the Booth Hall Childrens' Hospital, Blackley, were woken by the noise, and immediately recognised it as one they knew all too well. Several cried out that it was a doodlebug and told everyone to take cover under the beds.

Radcliffe received a drop of propaganda letters just before 06.00, but there were no casualties from the V1.

In Chapel Street, Tottington, near Bury, there was another serious incident. A V1 destroyed a row of terraced houses opposite St Anne's Church, at 05.50. Six people died and fourteen were injured, with one dying later. It took ten hours to remove the casualties. Clothes, bedding, and furnishings were blown into the trees of the churchyard, like grotesque Christmas decorations, and the church had most of its windows shattered. The vicar was one of the first rescuers to reach the scene; he held a Christmas Day service as usual the next day, despite the damage to the building. There is now a plaque in the Memorial Garden which carries the names of those who died.

A married couple, Nicholas (aged 50) and Mary Ann (aged 48) Conway died at 19 Chapel Street; their 22-year-old daughter Mary was seriously injured. Next door, Annie Greenhalgh, aged 75, died at the scene; her brother Dewhurst, aged 69, was injured and his wife Bertha, a health visitor, died of her injuries almost two months later, on 20 February, aged 64. Elizabeth Draper (aged 56), a shop assistant, died at number 31. James (aged 52) and Teresa (aged 56) Dyson, a married couple from Bulwell, had arrived a few hours before to spend Christmas with Teresa's sister Mary Rooney, a nurse; the couple both died but Mary was on duty at Bury Infirmary that night so was away from home. She later returned to help with the rescue effort. A total of 14 people were injured and taken to the Infirmary. Fifty-three people were made homeless. 27 houses were seriously damaged. This was the second worst incident of the Christmas Eve raid.

The other three V1s to land in Lancashire did not cause any serious casualties. At Gregson Lane, Brindle, near Chorley, three adults and a child had minor injuries; the V1 hit a chicken farm at about 05.28 and killed 30 birds, which may have caused additional food shortages, in view of the timing just before Christmas. 112 houses and two pubs were damaged, and some leaflets were found. Turton and Oswaldtwistle were also hit, but with no major injuries. Fragments of pamphlets were found at Turton.

In Derbyshire, there were three V1s. One destroyed a hedge at Beighton, damaged a farm and broke windows in about 150 buildings, while another killed a sheep at Plex Farm near Buxton, but there were no human casualties.

Nottinghamshire had only one V1, which exploded in a ploughed field at Sturton le Steeple. A small brown paper parcel containing copies of "Signal" magazine was found.

In Lincolnshire, there were two V1s; one damaged 40 houses at Epworth and another detonated in a field at Redbourne but there were otherwise no casualties.

Yorkshire had seven bombs. At Grange Moor, near Huddersfield, about 130 houses were damaged. The ARP report said laconically "no fatalities but massive structural damage" (West Riding ARP). One person had minor injuries and a cow was killed. The V1 at

Midhope Moor exploded in uninhabited moorland; Willerby had some damage to property and one slight casualty. At Barmby Moor near Pocklington the V1 fell into a gravel pit near the airfield, which contained much of the blast. 30 houses were damaged and a nearby Halifax aircraft was written off. A V1 brought down an overhead telephone line at Rossington, which disrupted communications for a time, while at the villages of North and South Cliffe there was minor damage.

The worst incident for Yorkshire was when a V1 wrecked a farm at Hubberton Green, Sowerby Bridge; it fell just behind Little Toothill Farm. The explosion blew the farmer, John Carter, out of bed, and the house was so damaged that he and his wife Mary had to move out. The V1 also contained propaganda leaflets, some still in their packages, and some chickens were killed by the blast.

The Carters had already lost their younger son in WW1. Willie (1893-1917) was serving with the 2nd Battalion Grenadier Guards when he was killed in Belgium on 31 July 1917 at the Battle of Pilckem Ridge. Selwyn, the elder son, was a farmer like his father and lived at Sod Farm, nearby. John and Mary moved in with him after the V1 incident. However, Mary never recovered from the bombing, and it was at her son's farm that she died some six months later, after suffering "permanent injuries". John Carter died in 1948, aged 80, having lost his son and his wife in two successive world wars.

County Durham had just one bomb. This, the furthest north of the 31, fell on Tudhoe Colliery cricket ground near Spennymoor at 06.05; apparently it blew up in mid-air, above roof level. The air raid siren had given advance warning and people were advised to take cover under the stairs, always the safest place. The V1 caused significant damage to property, shattering over a thousand windows and seriously injuring a man and three women. Another seven people were also injured; a vicarage, two churches, an orphanage and 390 houses were damaged. The boys of St Mary's Orphanage helped to clear up the mess. "There were a lot of ruined Christmas presents and [food] full of glass, but there was a tremendous spirit, too. We were winning at the time, we just got on with it."

The news was strictly censored, the *Northern Echo* on December 27 reported merely that the V1 had landed in a field in the north of England and that the orphanage boys had calmly helped to clear up the mess.

In Shropshire, there was just one bomb, at Newport, which damaged some plate glass windows. It fell quite far south and west from Manchester, almost as far south as Woodford, Northamptonshire, to the east, where another V1 exploded in a field, causing some damage to buildings but no casualties.

The V1s fell between 05.28 and 06.25.

The weekly summary by No 5 AA Group stated:

"In the early hours of Christmas Eve, the enemy launched his first attack against the North Midlands. The enemy himself has said that the target was Manchester and whilst this may have been the intended target, in fact the 28 [sic] incidents were scattered over nine counties.

"It was originally estimated that about 70 flying bombs were launched, but after a more detailed survey and taking into account the number of incidents over land, it is now considered that the number was about 40 [sic – actually more like 31 made landfall].

"Main landfall was across the Humber mouth between Spurn and Mablethorpe. Humber guns engaged seven targets."

There was a spread of 170 miles between the furthest north at Spennymoor and the furthest south at Woodford. 19 of the 31 V1s landed within a 30-mile radius of Manchester, but only 6 were 10 miles away. As has been stated before the V1s were not an especially accurate weapon, and the air launched V1s were harder to aim efficiently than their original counterparts. On this occasion, despite the plans for the raids, they failed to hit the city of Manchester itself. When you read accounts of the incidents, there was a general sense of disbelief and shock. This was the only time that so many counties in the North and Midlands had even seen a V1. The death toll could have been far worse as so many of the flying bombs fell in open countryside, but for those people who were woken early on Christmas Eve, it must have been terrifying.

Chapter 11

Christmas 1944 and After: The Last of the VIs

Christmas came and went. There were no further raids in the North of England, but the residents must have feared there could be. Nobody had expected a V1 raid on Christmas Eve; now, suddenly, it was entirely possible that there would be a new series of attacks, with more night-time raids just before dawn. The Government had to consider it as a distinct possibility. Should the defences be moved northwards again? The heavy falls of snow after Christmas that continued into the New Year must have made life even more difficult for people in the North.

The raids had caused repercussions and demonstrated that the Civil Defence services needed to be kept in a state of operational efficiency. The War Office finally gave permission to deploy anti-aircraft guns further north; 60 Heavy AA guns were moved up, then 4 Light AA troops. All of this took place in terrible weather but by December 29 all was almost complete, ready to engage the flying bombs that never came back. Hitler remarked that the Christmas Eve attack was worthwhile by "causing continual disturbance". He may well have had a point.

The aftermath of the Christmas Eve raid

In Abbey Hills Road, Oldham, 36 houses had been wrecked. 38 serious casualties from that raid were being treated in Oldham Royal Infirmary; some suffered life-changing injuries and would never make a full recovery. Others less severely injured would probably have been recovering at home (if they had a home to go to, that is). 27 people were homeless and spent Christmas Day, and perhaps several others following, in an Oldham rest centre. Many others went to stay with relatives. It was a close-knit community and many people simply moved from their damaged homes to stay with people nearby. Others, shaken by the raid, moved elsewhere. Those in London and the southeast had experienced the 1944 V1 attacks and recognised the (to them) familiar noises and the sudden silence; they knew to take cover. For the inhabitants of Abbey Hills Road, it had not been "just" a V1, but the first one they'd ever experienced. There was a further alert in Rochdale on 27 December, but this turned out to be a false alarm.

In Tottington 6 people were killed in a row of cottages, with one dying of her injuries the following February. Fourteen were injured and taken to Bury Infirmary. A nearby school was opened as an emergency centre for the 53 people made homeless, before friends and family offered them somewhere to stay. The vicar of St Anne's held services on Christmas Day in the badly damaged church. Despite the bitter cold, people attended to give thanks for their survival; 350 homes had been damaged.

With the help of their neighbours, people started to clear up the damage. The Christmas food that had already been put out ready for the celebrations was sprinkled with plaster and glass, but what was possible was rescued. Everywhere was covered with dust; for example, on Christmas Eve five mobile canteens had been needed in Oldham, because of all the fine powdered dust that kept clogging the rescuers' throats.

After Christmas, the burial of the dead began. Many funerals were on Friday 29 December. People continued to succumb to their injuries, even as late as February 1945.

While Oldham and Tottington were the main areas for significant injuries from the V1s, others were also affected. At Westwood Farm,

Hyde, the farmer and his family had been preparing for Christmas when the doodlebug hit the back of the farmhouse. The farmer's mother was sleeping there and was killed, along with her grandson. The farmer, his wife and daughter spent Christmas in hospital; when they came home, they were appalled to discover the farm had been looted. The farmer was already distressed by the loss of his dairy cattle in the raid and decided to give up farming.

Within a few hours of the attack on Manchester, Air Chief Marshal Sir Roderic Hill had authorised the removal of sixty heavy guns from the East coast gun-belt to reinforce North Sea defences, between Filey and Skegness. Two days later, four troops of light AA guns and some searchlight detachments moved north to join them. They travelled through thick fog and frost, with heavy snow along the Yorkshire coast. By 29 December the new defences were almost complete. Sir Roderic immediately ordered the guns to be deployed north of the Wash. In fact, there were to be no further bombs in the North, and three weeks later the German air launching unit ceased operations altogether.

There were no more V1 attacks until the start of the New Year. The main issue was lack of fuel. Once KG 53 received a fuel allocation for the first raid of 1945, the air launched bombing could resume. Meanwhile "Operation Vapour" began. The Fighter Interception Development Squadron (of the Night Fighter Development Wing) carried out operational trials at RAF Ford and later Manston under the code name of Operation Vapour; these were to use ASV radar to detect and destroy the Heinkels and their V1s. A Coastal Command Wellington with ASV would patrol up and down at very low level along the Dutch coast; it would be accompanied by a Mosquito or Beaufighter or both, one to get the Heinkel and the other the V1 if it had already been launched. They would wait until the target was picked up on radar and would then go for the kill. The idea was that continuous patrols could be made round the clock.

As January 1945 began, hope grew in England that the end of the war would soon arrive. The V1 flying bombs were now far less common although the V2 rockets remained a serious threat. (It is surprisingly difficult to provide reliable information about the last phase of the attacks in 1945 because often accounts simply assumed any explosion was caused by a V2.) Despite all the challenges, air-launched V1s reached London on a further four occasions in January before the campaign ground to a halt; they caused significant damage, including deaths and serious injuries.

The air launch raids begin again, January 1945

The evening of Wednesday 3 January 1945 was to be the last large-scale raid carried out by air-launched Heinkels. There were two attacks carried out very close together; they lasted from about 18.30 to 20.25, one of the longest recent air launched V1 raids. The Heinkels launched forty-five V1s, roughly the same number as during the Christmas Eve attack. As on that occasion, a number of launches (seventeen in this case) were aborted and nineteen were shot down by AA fire. Eleven of these V1s (AA) were shot down over the sea. Three Heinkels were accidentally lost during the operation.

The V1s that fell on land caused a variety of damage, mainly to property in Suffolk, Essex and Norfolk; at Aldeburgh at 18.35, thirteen houses were damaged. At Ellough, the church and thirteen houses were affected by blast. Tendring had a ten-ton stack of straw set on fire and destroyed, despite the NFS's attempts to put it out. At Hopton another thirteen houses were damaged. There was a large crater and minor damage to twenty houses at Hempnall. A bungalow was wrecked at North Weald. High Ongar and Langham were among other places affected. Two people were seriously injured at Bredfield, Suffolk. One missile made it as far as Lewisham at 20.14, only four minutes after the alert, falling on allotments and severely damaging four houses but with no recorded casualties. Comparing this raid with that of Christmas Eve in terms of size, the casualties might have been far more serious. However, it was proof that the V1 threat still existed; random V1s could still reach London, as the 5 January attacks would confirm.

There was another attack during the late evening of Friday 5 January. This was short, little more than fifteen minutes, and lasted between about 22.10 and 22.25; however, its consequences were serious for both sides. Four Heinkels were lost: two shot down and two in accidents. Ten missiles were launched; five of them were aborted and two were downed by anti-aircraft fire. The remaining three all reached London and caused considerable damage. One hit Fairfield Road, Beckenham at 22.26, only three minutes after the alert; it killed twelve people and seriously injured twenty-two, with severe damage to about forty houses nearby. Christ Church was badly damaged and there was minor damage to a further 150 houses and shops. In Lambeth, three minutes later, a V1 hit the south side of Fentiman Road; this killed fourteen people and seriously injured thirty-six, with some damage to property. A rescue dog had to be brought in to search for survivors in the rubble and a hundred people were made homeless. There was also a direct hit on Roding Lane, Wanstead, and several houses were wrecked, but with no serious casualties. With twenty-six deaths in all and fifty-eight injured, these were the worst of the January attacks.

On the night of 12/13 January there was a small raid between 06.00 and 07.00. Of the five V1s launched, two were aborted and another two were shot down. A V1 at Chapel St Andrew, Suffolk, failed to detonate and the bomb disposal team experienced some considerable difficulty in extricating it from a cesspool.

The final air-launched raid took place on the night of 13/14 January. It lasted from 01.35 to 02.05. Twenty-five flying bombs were launched; ten were aborted and seven were shot down by AA, with one shot down by a fighter. Seven got through, six of which fell on London. One of them was believed to be carrying propaganda leaflets; a single leaflet headed "The Other Side" was found in Gravesend and is believed to have come from one of the two missiles that landed in Orpington. There must have been other leaflets that fell with it but it is thought that these may have been recovered by private individuals. This leaflet is thought to have been the last in the air-launched propaganda war.

The worst incident of this raid was when a doodlebug made a direct hit on terraced houses in Horsman Street, Southwark, at 01.55, destroying thirty houses and badly damaging another hundred. Ten people were killed and seventeen seriously injured. Vera Verrey, aged 20, her brother Albert, aged 17, and their parents Thomas, aged 68 and Ellen, aged 61, all died in the incident, at 11 Horsman Street. Beatrice Glenister, aged 68, from number 12, John Press, aged 65, from number 14, and William (62) and Marion (64) Rogers and Maud Callagham (61), all from number 16, also died in this incident. These were the last deaths from this stage of the air-launched campaign.

Most of the other V1s caused damage to property but no loss of life. The other London targets were Orpington (twice), Mitcham, Hornsey and Enfield. AA fire exploded a V1 over Southwold, injuring a soldier. The final air-launched V1 to hit Britain exploded on the ground in Hornsey at 02.13 on 14 January.

The crippling fuel shortage made it impossible for the flights to continue; in addition, combat losses, both from prematurely exploding V1s and from attacks by Allied fighters, meant that there were no longer enough viable aircraft to mount a significant air-launched attack. As a result, KG 53's air launched campaign ended on 14 January 1945.

The next stage of the V1 campaign: developing a longer-range flying bomb

If air-launched V1s were no longer a possibility, how else could flying bombs reach England? The next step for the Germans was to consider increasing the range of the ramp-launched V1s, so that the missiles could reach London from ramps at ground sites in German-occupied territory in western Holland. This involved a change in design; the new V1 was longer, lighter and with a smaller warhead. This F-1 version was made slightly longer (about 30 feet, rather than 27 feet) and lighter, with a larger fuel tank. Plywood was used in the construction of the wings and nose cone to cut down the weight and the warhead was lighter; myrol was used for the explosive filling. Twenty-three small incendiary bombs were added to balance the missile. Other aspects of performance were tweaked, so that eventually the modified missile had a range of 200 miles, rather than the original 150. This meant that the new V1s could reach London from ramps at sites in the Netherlands, rather than relying on access to bases near the French Channel coast, as they had been able to do the previous summer.

Once the design had been agreed, it was time to build sufficient longer-range V1s so that a large-scale attack could be launched. Ideally this would have been done to coincide with the Battle of the Bulge Offensive, during the period 16 December 1944-late January 1945. However, there were delays; these included those caused by the bombing of the factories producing the missiles, logistical problems and shortage of steel. As a result, the longer-range V1s could not be delivered until later in February or March 1945. Allied intelligence realised that the design was changing when they found fragments of some of the V1s fired into Belgium that month.

On 25 February 1945, the Air Ministry warned the Chiefs of Staff that the UK was once again vulnerable to flying bomb attacks. They ordered an air reconnaissance survey of the German-occupied areas of the Netherlands. Bletchley's photographic interpreters found two ramps almost at once and issued a warning the following day that attacks by longer range flying bombs were imminent. The evidence showed that two launching sites were being developed, one at

Ypenburg near the Hague and one at Vlaardingen, west of Rotterdam. (There was a third near Delft, which came into use on 9 March but was not spotted by the British till later.)

Resuming the V1 attacks

On Friday 2 March, the V1 attacks began once more, this time from the three land-launched sites in the Netherlands, as described above.

Air Chief Marshal Sir Roderic Hill and General Pile promptly changed the defences, moving ninety-six heavy guns from the northern areas to between the Isle of Sheppey and Orford Ness, along with some training batteries. By Tuesday 6 March these were all in position, and fighter units were also reorganised to meet the new threat. 83 Squadron of Second Tactical Air Force (2 TAF) began to attack the two known launch sites in the Netherlands from 2 March onwards.

The *Daily Telegraph* of 4 March reported that "The Germans... resumed attacks on this country with flying bomb(s)...It is believed that flying bombs that crossed the coast have come from land launching sites much more distant than any previously used."

In the first few hours of the raid on Friday morning, 2 March, thirteen flying bombs appeared on the radar, but only seven were within range of the defences. Six were shot down and the seventh came down at Neptune Street, Bermondsey at 03.07. A block of flats suffered slight blast damage, but there were no casualties. These were the first flying bombs from the new ramps in southwest Holland.

On the Saturday morning 3 March, a bomb was shot down by AA fire over Walton Cliffs; it hit Frinton at 04.56 and was found to contain incendiary bombs. A further eight missiles came over at intervals; only four made landfall. Two hit Cuffley (home of the 1916 Zeppelin crash) and Stapleford, while one hit London, in Noel Park, Wood Green at 16.09 (Farrant Avenue, Lordship Lane). It killed seven people; rescue dogs were used to search the wreckage. (This incident was wrongly attributed to a V2 in some accounts.)

On Sunday 4 March a further three V1s arrived. They fell at Redbourne, near Luton, Camberwell/Dulwich (at 10.44) and Addlestone Road, Chertsey (at 10.47). There was also an earlier airburst over Plough Way, Rotherhithe, at 05.40, with some damage but no casualties.

There were more doodlebugs on Monday 5 March; ten were detected, five of which made landfall. One was shot down by AA fire at Foulness, while the other four reached London in late morning, at Barnet, Barking (11.06), Bermondsey/Rotherhithe (11.20) and Whitewebbs Road, Enfield (12.32). The V1 which hit Swedish Yard in Rotherhithe at 11.20 badly damaged the top two floors of a four-storey warehouse. A railway pumping station was also damaged. One person was injured.

There were two more sets of V1 attacks that week. On Tuesday 6 March, eight V1s were detected, but most were shot down. The four that fell on land were in Essex and near Margate. Two days later, on Thursday 8 March, three more V1s were detected, but all were shot down. No casualties were reported on either day.

There was then a gap until Wednesday 14 March, when six V1s were detected by UK radar. Five were shot down, but one hit Northolt. This was the V1 which hit the Royal Army Ordnance Depot at 09.23, causing fourteen civilian and military deaths and injuring more than a hundred and ten people. Four dead were from the Royal Army Ordnance Corps and two from the ATS; the remaining eight were civilians, including Lizzie Maud Swift and Alice Hilda Isitt who lived locally and were thought to be working at the Ordnance Depot. One casualty was the workshop handyman who had been walking past the building with the morning tea trolley when the V1 exploded on the store shed. Building 413 was the point of impact, according to the RAOC history; another account suggests building 416. This account mentions the surreal aftermath of the explosion. The store had contained a large number of recoil springs for 25 pounder guns, each one about 1.5 metres long and 200mm in diameter: these dispersed everywhere, probably bouncing away after the explosion. This was arguably the last V1 to cause casualties in the London area, though V1s got as far as Paddington on 24 March and Orpington on the 26th.

The next day four more V1s were detected; one fell short and the remaining three were shot down over the sea.

On Friday 16 March, only one V1 was detected, but it was to have serious consequences. It exploded at 05.35 at Morland Avenue, Dartford; it killed four people and injured twenty-seven. It also damaged over 450 houses, which is probably why so many accounts insist that the explosion must have been a V2. Eyewitnesses spoke of the large amounts of broken glass everywhere and the blaze of a gas main on fire. These were the last confirmed deaths caused by a V1 in England.

One of those affected was Keith Richards, later to become famous as a musician and guitarist with the Rolling Stones. He was only a baby at the time, little more than a year old, living with his family in Morland Avenue. Their house suffered bomb damage in this raid and the family had to move elsewhere, further up the road to where Keith's aunt lived.

During the period March 3-16, 1945, there were 14 incidents where the bombs were not destroyed by AA fire. These could be regarded as a mere postscript to the main campaign, but probably did not appear as such to anyone living on the East coast or London at the time. Although the death rate was far less than the previous year, people were still being randomly bombed out of their homes or indeed killed while sheltering in them.

Over the weekend there were sporadic V1s. Only one made landfall out of the four launched; it hit Somersham in the early hours of Saturday morning, 17 March, but with no casualties. (There is a reference to it "causing damage to 190" but I have been unable to substantiate this, still less establish whether the number refers to damaged properties or people.) Two more V1s came over on the Sunday, but both were shot down over the sea.

On Monday 19 March, nine V1s were detected on radar but only four got through. One hit Harlow at 05.47. The three others were later: Shipbourne at 08.12, Sutton Valence at 09.14 and Thornham Parva at 09.16, the latter with some damage to property and 21 incendiary bombs found. On Tuesday, Wednesday and Thursday a few more were detected, but with no serious consequences. Two were detected on Tuesday and both were shot down over the sea; on Wednesday three were detected and all were shot down. Thursday's attack was larger; twelve V1s were detected, of which two fell short and nine were shot down over the sea. One was shot down on land and fell next to Frinton golf course, leaving burnt out incendiary bombs behind. (Clearly the new design of V1 was including incendiaries as part of its payload.) On Friday 23, six were detected; three fell short, one was shot down but one of the remainder fell at Eltham, Kent, causing damage to property, including a railway station.

That week RAF Typhoons bombed the V1 launch site at Vlaardingen on 23 March, while on 20 and 23 March Spitfires bombed the second site at Ypenburg. Essential parts of both sites were destroyed, and it became clear that the end of the campaign was approaching. From then on it would be down to the launch site at Delft to deliver the final V1s.

The next weekend saw further sporadic V1s. On Saturday 24 March one reached Paddington at 07.57 but caused no serious damage. On Sunday 25 fourteen were detected, but only two got through. One injured eight people in Lowdells Lane, East Grinstead, just before 08.00, along with widespread damage to housing. Another fell in Dagenham at 02.32.

On Monday 26 March, nine V1s were detected but the only two that evaded the defences fell at Chelsham, Surrey and Orpington (05.25). There were no casualties. On Tuesday 27 March, ten were detected but nine of these were shot down. One fell at North Cray, with no casualties. (This was the final day of the V2 campaign, see below.) The next day, fifteen V1s were detected and thirteen were shot down. Of the remainder, one fell at Chislehurst at 07.54, the other at Waltham Holy Cross at 07.55.

The final batch of V1s began at 21.30 on Wednesday 28 March; these were launched from Delft, the last remaining site, and this continued into Thursday 29 March. Twelve V1s were detected. Three fell short, four were shot down over the sea and four shot down over land. At 08.56 one crashed near a sewage farm at Datchworth, Hertfordshire, damaging six houses; this was the last V1 to land and explode on British soil. At 09.59 that morning, the penultimate V1 sent towards England was downed by anti-aircraft guns at Iwade, near Sittingbourne; it fell only a few miles away from the first V1 of the campaign, which had landed in Kent at Swanscombe on 13 June 1944. The final V1 flying bomb of the war was shot down into the sea off Orford Ness by the highly effective Orford Ness DIVER anti-aircraft gun battery at 12.43, 29 March.

The three new launch sites had launched 275 missiles altogether between 2 and 29 March, but only 160 came close enough to be detected by UK-based radar. 31 of these evaded UK defences and only 13 reached as far as London. They caused 32 deaths and over 130 injuries. Perhaps not a large number of casualties, especially if you look back to the raids and casualties of 30 June the previous year, to give just one example, but still somehow shocking at that point in the war, especially as quite a few of the V1s came over in daylight, at a time when people were going to work or going shopping and were hoping that at this stage it would be safe to do this. The V1 remained a terror weapon, right to the end.

This was the end of the campaign, after more than nine months. It had lasted far longer than the so-called "doodlebug summer" and involved a range of methods of attack: initial sites in France, modified sites in France and elsewhere, air-launched sites, attacks in Europe, attacks involving propaganda, modified V1s and attacks using ramps again in the Netherlands. A long and challenging campaign, to be examined in the next chapter.

The last of the V2s

It should not be forgotten that the V2s continued to arrive throughout March 1945 and there were several deadly incidents, some with a far higher death toll than the last V1 attacks. While it was generally accepted that the war was coming to an end, the civilian population, especially in London, continued to fear that they might die from the last rockets of the campaign.

At 11.10 on Thursday 8 March, a V2 at Smithfield Market resulted in 110 dead, 123 seriously injured and 243 with lesser injuries. The market was packed with traders and customers. Almost two weeks later, at 09.39 on Wednesday 21 March, not long after the start of the working day, a V2 hit the Packard factory on the Great West Road, Brentford; it also damaged twelve other factories nearby. 32 people were killed then or died soon afterwards, and 500 were injured.

The worst incident that March was at 07.21 on Tuesday the 27th, when a V2 made a direct hit on Hughes Mansions, Vallance Road, Stepney. It fell in the middle of an estate of five-storey flats. 134 or 135 people died and 43 were seriously injured. Many of the victims were children who were getting ready for school; some of them had only recently returned from being evacuated.

Rescuers were still extricating the wounded from the wreckage that afternoon when the final V2 of the war landed in Orpington at 16.37. It hit Kynaston Road, injuring about 70 people. 34-year-old Ivy Millichamp was killed at number 88. Her husband pulled her from the wreckage, but she was already dead. This was the last death from a V2 on British soil.

The V2 rocket assault had seen a total of 1,115 fall on England, of which 517 fell on London. They killed 2,754 people and injured 6,523. (These statistics vary from source to source, but this gives a general indication.)

What next?

Now that the V1 and V2 attacks had ended, what next? Colonel Wachtel was still reluctant to admit defeat. On 9 April Vere Hodgson remarked in her diary *Few Eggs and No Oranges* that Notting Hill had received no bombs for more than a week. She was delighted to be able to go to bed in peace, without the fear of explosions or the roof collapsing. As she said, no one knows what it means unless they have lived with it. Millions of Londoners would have agreed with her, as would the inhabitants of Doodlebug Alley.

However, by mid-April, Flak Regt 155 (W) had ceased work. The German Air Force Depot at Karwitz, which was known to have supplied flying bombs for the London attacks, had been evacuated on about 8 April. Bletchley had warned that the Germans were still trying to bring into use a modified V1 by mid-April. It was to have an increased range of 310 miles but a reduced explosive charge of 882 pounds; the normal charge was 1840 pounds. It was thought Antwerp would be the main target. However, the evacuation of Flak Regiment 155 (W), presumably to fight at the front, meant the end of any further attempts to launch flying bombs, whether by ramp or by other methods. All other possibilities, whether it might be larger/smaller V1s, piloted V1s (as suggested by Hanna Reitsch and her idea for "Operation Suicide") or even possible attacks on the United States via submarine-launched V1s, came to nothing.

Colonel Wachtel retreated to Luneberg but on 4 May all the troops there surrendered unconditionally to Montgomery. Four days later the war in Europe was over.

Chapter 12

Conclusion: Looking Back

Norman Longmate, in his excellent work on the Doodlebugs, states that the battle of the flying bomb was won by the Allies; I agree with his conclusions, though I might take issue with his choice of verb. The campaign did not achieve its targets, even though it went on for far longer than originally expected: over nine months rather than the ten-week "doodlebug summer" that is frequently described in histories of the Second World War. People went on being bombed, dying, losing their homes both at home and abroad well into the spring of 1945. The development of the V1 failed to delay the Normandy landings and did not change the Allies' overall strategy. It may have improved German morale, at least in the beginning, but it did not force the Allies to negotiate a peaceful settlement, as had originally been hoped. It was undoubtedly a terror weapon, and an indiscriminate one; it might lack accuracy but was still fully capable of killing or injuring at random. The population of London and the southeast was significantly affected; when you talk about World War Two to those who lived through it in London, it's very often the doodlebug campaign that stands out, even more than the 1940/41 Blitz, especially the noise, followed by the dramatic silence and then an explosion within seconds. That sequence seemed to be ingrained in people's memories, and many still talk of it to this day, even when they were not directly affected or living in the immediate vicinity.

However, it could be said that the V1 itself was a "remarkable achievement" (Norman Longmate, *The Doodlebugs*, p. 473). It was a remarkably cheap weapon and cost next to nothing in terms of German lives lost. (Apart from the "friendly fire" effect when some of the later ramp-launched V1s fell back on the Germans trying to launch them.) Given that the V1s were often built by slave labour and the death toll among this group was significant, this should also be taken into account. Possibly as many as 20,000 died making the V1s; many more died making them than the numbers of civilians killed by them, a terrible contrast that is all too often ignored. Tens of thousands of civilians from occupied Europe were forced to work for the Nazis and were subjected to starvation, torture and even execution while doing so.

The financial cost is hard to establish. RAE Farnborough suggested the V1s could be built for about £115 each (1944 prices) with a large-scale contract. The German government's contract with Volkswagen allowed for a slightly higher average cost of about £125. One of the German propaganda leaflets gave a figure of £600, but this is perhaps in contrast with the cost of a Lancaster that they gave: £60,000. Perhaps the overall cost was about £150 per V1. The Air Ministry, in a secret report in November 1944, suggested that the enemy's costs were less than a quarter of that of the Allies. In the initial V1 offensive, from 12 June to 1 September, the cost to the Allies was thought to be in the region of £48 million. This covered aircraft and men lost, bombs dropped, shells fired, and balloons lost. The cost of replacing destroyed and damaged housing was at least £25 million and by the autumn that had risen to about £62 million, although this included some V2 damage from September onwards. After that the V1 costs gradually tailed off, though they were still significant. By the end of the war, the costs must have been getting on for £70 million. In contrast, up to 1 September, the Germans were thought to have incurred costs of about £12,600,000: building launch sites, training crews and building the missiles themselves. Even when you include the costs of the large numbers of Heinkels (possibly as many as 77) lost during the main air launch campaign, the odds are very much in the Germans' favour. Norman Longmate's estimate was that for every £1 a V1 cost the Germans, the British taxpayer paid £5.

The death toll shows a similar contrast. Again, the V1 campaign favoured the Germans in terms of fatal casualties. By February 1945, Colonel Wachtel's men had only lost 185 victims (including deaths in accidents, of which there were many); 2,900 Allied airmen had died, including those who died in the attacks on Peenemünde. Several hundred Allied servicemen were killed by V1s on the ground. (The Guards' Chapel and Imber Court incidents are just two examples.)

In total, 6,184 civilians and 2,917 servicemen (to include V2 casualties for the servicemen abroad in Antwerp and elsewhere) died during the campaign. (These figures are approximate.) 17,981 civilians and 1,939 servicemen (again, including V2 here) were seriously injured. More than 23,000 houses in England were totally destroyed and more than a million were damaged; many of these later had to be rebuilt. Approximately 5,582 people were killed in the London boroughs, including 207 service personnel. Croydon had some of the worst casualties outside central London; 211 residents were killed, 697 seriously wounded and 1,277 needed medical treatment during the nine-month campaign.

It is hard to establish numbers of V1s by area as it is rare that the numbers tally when different accounts are considered; many of the tables available tend to cover dates until October 1944, while others also include V2 for all of WW2. Over 10,400 V1s were launched from June 1944 to March 1945; about 9,251 of these were fired against London. (The phrase "fired against" is an attempt to cover the intention rather than the actual effect of the attacks.) Many flying bombs went off course, landed in the sea or were shot down over water. About 25% failed to cross the Channel or the North Sea, 7,488 crossed the south coast, of which 3,957 were shot down.

A total of 5,823 V1 incidents was reported to the Civil Defence authorities as taking place on land. Probably this number is underreported as some may have fallen in remote areas and might not have been logged. Up to the end of August 1944, 2,242 landed in London about 41% of the total. About another 80 or more hit

Greater London between then and the end of March 1945. (Bob Ogley suggests 2,419 for London in this earlier part of the campaign, basing his estimate on drawings from RAF draughtsmen.) All the Greater London boroughs experienced at least one V1; no borough escaped attack. Croydon had the most, with 141 V1s, followed by Wandsworth with 122 and Lewisham with 114. Generally, the boroughs to the south and east of the Thames had higher totals, many in the 70-80 range of flying bombs; Camberwell, Woolwich, Greenwich, Lambeth, Beckenham and Orpington each received over fifty V1s. West Ham was the worst borough north of the river with 58. Logically one might suppose that central London was the main target. Yet Westminster, home to the Guards' Chapel, suffered only 29 V1 attacks. Twickenham, which had six V1s in one day on 19 June had only 27 doodlebugs in total, a similar number to Westminster. The V1 that affected my grandparents in Acton was one of only seven in the borough, while Richmond had eight.

It is easy to imagine that London bore the brunt of the flying bombs; after all, Hitler had frequently stated that this was his intention. However, the areas described as "Doodlebug Alley" also paid a heavy price. Kent received 1,444 V1s, with a further thousand shot down over the sea; 448 communities were damaged, some affected more than once. One hundred and one doodlebugs were shot down over Kent in the first week alone; after that the incidents averaged about 20 a day during the peak of the campaign. Although the area was far less densely populated than central London, at least 156 people were killed and 1,716 were injured.

Sussex was hit by 886 V1s. This figure excludes those shot down by coastal defences, fighters and AA guns. Surrey had only 295, possibly because some missiles fell short. The east coast of the UK also suffered V1 attacks in smaller numbers, from Yorkshire (7) through Norfolk (13) with Suffolk (93) and Essex (412); the latter two were significantly affected by the change in focus of the air launch programme. Essex, rather than Kent, became the final "Doodlebug

Alley", while Suffolk's attacks were largely in the autumn and winter. Hertfordshire had 82. Hampshire (including the Isle of Wight) had 80 V1 attacks, largely because of the raids on Southampton and Portsmouth. The Christmas Eve raid meant that Lancashire, Cheshire, Yorkshire, Derbyshire, Lincolnshire, Nottinghamshire, Shropshire, Northamptonshire and County Durham all received small numbers of V1s. In all, twenty-five of the then forty counties of England had been subjected to at least one V1. Only western counties, notably Herefordshire, Worcestershire, Gloucestershire (this despite Germany's best efforts against Gloucester), Wiltshire, Dorset, Somerset, Devon and Cornwall avoided any attack by the flying bombs. Wales, Scotland and Northern Ireland did not receive any either.

Even today, there are still many scars on the landscape that provide clues to that nine-month period. Buildings were frequently rebuilt as before, for example in Priory Road Hounslow, where the bombed houses were rebuilt in the same style sometime after the war (1947 or after). Sometimes you can see a gap in a row of terraced houses, or a change in architecture. There are plenty of craters in the countryside where V1s were shot down or fell short of their targets. It is still possible, for example, to locate where the Otford V1 fell on 30 June, and many of the Christmas Eve V1s that fell outside built-up areas can be located by the craters left behind.

I have tried to include firsthand accounts, when possible, to suggest what life was like during the protracted "doodlebug summer" and afterwards. Everyday life went on, despite the raids, but many of the accounts indicate quite how terrifying things were. Even simply the reintroduction of schemes for evacuation of the vulnerable suggests how the V1 campaign made it advisable for children to leave home yet again; for some of them it would have been the third time since 1939, with the September 1939 evacuation followed by the London Blitz of 1940. The casualty figures are shocking; while definitions of specific types of "severe" and "slight" injuries are not given, "severe" is usually defined as requiring hospital treatment and "slight" as treated at a first aid post. Many people were left with lasting scars, physical or mental, that they retained for the rest of their lives. Others who lost their homes lost many of their possessions in the process; what is not often recorded is the effects the various experiences had on those who survived. So many memories were destroyed during the raids; so many cherished household items were lost when houses were damaged. Often, the minutiae of everyday life went missing in the attacks, scattered by blast or simply looted. Possessions, photographs, certificates, keepsakes and all the documents that go to represent a life just no longer existed for the survivors. There were many acts of bravery, both military and civilian, such as Captain Jean Maridor's valiant attempts to down doodlebugs, including his last-ditch attempt to prevent damage to Benenden hospital, where he lost his life. Many pilots sacrificed their lives to destroy V1s before these reached their targets. The AA batteries were also vulnerable to attack. Many air raid wardens died while trying to get people to safety; they were often the last to take shelter and the emergency services were often at the forefront of the action.

I hope this book provides not only an account of the V1 campaign but also pays tribute to all those who died in, or were affected by, the many incidents. I would like to pay tribute to all those who shared their experiences of this period, as well as to all those who died by enemy action. They will not be forgotten; we will remember them.

Bibliography

Books

Barnfield, Paul, *When the Bombs Fell: Twickenham, Teddington and the Hamptons under Aerial Bombardment during the Second World War* (Borough of Twickenham Local History Society, October 2001, reprinted 2007).

Bates, H.E., *Flying Bombs over England*, edited by Bob Ogley (Froglets Publications, 1994).

Campbell, Christy, *Target London* (Abacus, 2013).

Colledge, Maureen, *Tin hats, doodlebugs & food rations: memories of Acton in World War 2* (Acton History Group, 2014).

Cull, Brian with Lander, Bruce, *Diver! Diver! Diver!* (Grub Street, 2008).

Gardiner, Juliet, *Wartime: Britain 1939-1945* (Headline Review, 2005).

Gore, Jan, *Send More Shrouds: the V1 attack on the Guards' Chapel 1944* (Pen & Sword, 2017).

Hodgson, Vere, *Few Eggs and no Oranges* (Persephone, 1999.)

Jones, R.V., *Most Secret War: British Scientific Intelligence 1939-1945* (Hamish Hamilton, 1978).

Longmate, Norman, *The doodlebugs: the story of the flying bombs* (Hutchinson, 1981).

Morrison, Herbert (Lord Morrison of Lambeth), *An autobiography* (Odhams, 1960).

Ogley, Bob, *Doodlebugs and Rockets: the battle of the flying bomb* (Froglets Publications, 1992).

Sansom, William, *The Blitz: Westminster at war* (Oxford University Press, 1990).

Sheppard-Jones, Elisabeth, *I walked on wheels* (Geoffrey Bles, 1958).

Smith, Peter J. C., *Air-launched doodlebugs: the forgotten campaign* (Pen & Sword, 2006).

Smith, Peter J. C., *Flying Bombs over the Pennines: the story of the V-1 attack aimed at Manchester on December 24th 1944* (Neil Richardson, 1988).

Smith, Peter J. C., *Luftwaffe over Manchester* (Neil Richardson, 2003).

Thomas, Graham A., *Terror in the Sky: the Battle against the Flying Bombs* (Pen & Sword, 2008).

Upton, Dennis, *The Dangerous Years: life in Ealing, Acton and Southall in the Second World War 1939-45* (Dennis Upton, 1993).

Articles

Lewis, Keith, 'Surviving the flying bomb: death and destruction in the Guards' Chapel' in *The Grenadier Gazette*, 2001, no. 24, pp.42-43.

The National Archives:

Various, including:

Air 20/4128: Flying bombs – lists of incidents including those against London March 1945

AIR 20/4129 The last of the flying bombs (includes dates and time for March 1945 V1s)

AIR 40/2656 Flying bombs/ details of 111 KG3 and information on bombardment of Liège November 1944

HO 186/2360, AIR RAIDS, Major and minor bomb incidents: reports. 1939-1945

Websites

Account of the bombing at the Co-op Stores, Lordship Lane, 5 August 1944 by Mary Skinner https://www.dulwichsociety.com/newsletter/autumn-2005/life-changing-day

The Aldwych bomb, 30 June 1944, by Derrick Grady https://www.bbc.co.uk/history/ww2peopleswar/stories/32/a2036332.shtml

Brassey square incident, 17 July 1944 https://jamescousins.com/2010/10/brassey-square-bombing/index.html

Flying Bombs and Rockets (Stephen Henden): https://www.flyingbombsandrockets.com/

Material on Antwerp and the V1 and V2 campaign: http://www.v2rocket.com/start/chapters/antwerp.html

Also: https://assets.publishing.service.gov.uk/government/uploads/system/uploads/attachment_data/file/30058/ww2_antwerp.pdf

Also:List of those who died in the Rex Cinema, Antwerp, with some biographical details, compiled by Pieter Serrien : https://pieterserrien-be.translate.goog/slachtofferlijstcinemarex/

Oak Lane train crash, 18 August 1944: https://mikegunnill.tumblr.com/post/94429099769/the-70th-anniversary-oak-lane-train-crash

https://www.historicmedway.co.uk/localdisasters/v1_rainham_train_crash.htm gives another source for the Oak Lane crash.

The Sloane Court bombing. https://www.londonmemorial.org/, which gives more detail on the victims.

STC V1 at New Southgate: Doris Phillips' account of 23 August: https://www.bbc.co.uk/history/ww2peopleswar/stories/49/a1128449.shtml

Unpublished sources

Correspondence with Jenny A'Court about wartime Antwerp
Correspondence with Doreen Bull and her son John
Correspondence with Joy Hilder about the Otford V1

Index